GROWING INTO WHOLENESS

**Overseas Missionary
Fellowship
1058 Avenue Road
Toronto, Ontario M5N 2C6**

Growing Into Wholeness

Marion Ashton

A Falcon Book

KINGSWAY PUBLICATIONS
EASTBOURNE

ISBN 0 86065 404 4

Falcon Books
are published by Kingsway Publications
in conjunction with the Church Pastoral Aid Society,
an Anglican evangelical society committed to helping
local churches in mission and growth.
CPAS Mission at Home, Falcon Court,
32 Fleet Street, London EC4Y 1DB.

Front cover photo: Tony Stone Photolibrary — London

Printed in Great Britain for
KINGSWAY PUBLICATIONS LTD
Lottbridge Drove, Eastbourne, E. Sussex BN23 6NT by
Richard Clay (The Chaucer Press) Ltd, Bungay, Suffolk
Typeset by CST, Eastbourne, East Sussex.

CONTENTS

The author is grateful to Inter-Varsity Press, MacMillan & Co. Ltd, Epworth Press, Nisbet & Co. Ltd, Marshall Morgan & Scott Ltd, Hodder & Stoughton Ltd, Pickering & Inglis, Banner of Truth Trust, and SPCK for permission to reproduce short extracts from previously published works. (See *Notes* at the end of the book for details.)

ACKNOWLEDGEMENTS

I am most grateful to all those who have patiently read either part or the whole of what I have written. They have given most helpful and constructive criticism as well as repeated encouragement. I am also deeply grateful to the many who have prayed for me as I have written.

Particularly I wish to express my heartfelt thanks to Mary Read, who has done all the typing—from the first rough drafts, which involved deciphering my pencilled handwriting, to the final manuscript. She has also given me most valuable suggestions along the way, and sat with me as we read through the whole, before the final manuscript was submitted.

Frequently, my prayer when preparing to speak or teach has been:

> O teach me, Lord, that I may teach
> The precious things thou dost impart;
> And wing my words that they may reach
> The hidden depths of many a heart.
>
> *F. R. Havergal*

This is now my prayer for the written words in which I have tried to convey some of the precious truths the Lord has been teaching over the years, and which I am still seeking to learn.

I

INTRODUCTION

It Is God Who Makes Things Grow

The guest on the radio programme *Desert Island Discs* was being asked what item of luxury he would like to take to his desert island. His answer was that he would choose a potter's wheel. In explaining this choice he said, 'I'd just want to make things.'

As I listened, my mind immediately went to the scene described at the beginning of Jeremiah 18. God sent Jeremiah to the potter's house and he saw the potter working at the wheel. He was making a jar out of clay. Suddenly something went wrong, the jar was spoiled and it was not turning out at all as the potter intended. As he continued to watch he saw that instead of throwing away that lump of clay the potter was patiently and persistently working at remaking the jar. He was softening, moulding and reshaping the clay, until there grew in those skilful hands and through his control of the wheel a thing of beauty, of delight to his eyes, exactly as he wanted it to be.

I want to start there as we think about growing into wholeness. 'In the beginning God . . .' (Gen 1:1). God is the great Maker. Reverently we hear his voice echoing in eternity, 'I want to make things.' Of all the things that he has made, the greatest, the most wonderful is mankind, male and female—made in his image, in his likeness. And God is the Potter. It is God who takes into his hands this human material, made in his image yet so terribly spoiled, so unlike what he intended; and who persistently, continuously and patiently remakes it. It is God who causes it to grow into that wholeness, that completeness which he desires. Unless we start with God, we are likely to think of growing into wholeness as something we must strive to bring about, something we must achieve. Certainly, we are not passive in the process. We need to actively and wholeheartedly co-operate with God, but it is God with whom we are to co-operate; it is not God who is to co-operate with our efforts!

The New Testament in particular is full of the fact that this heavenly Potter who has us in his hands, moulding us and controlling the wheel of circumstances which helps to shape us, is also within us remaking us from within. Paul said, 'It is God who works in you' (Phil 2:13), and 'He who began a good work in you will carry it on to completion' (Phil 1:6). The more we grasp this the less we shall strive and the more we shall rest in the assurance of God's work in us. From time to time we may get glimpses of the fact that God really is at work in us, doing things which we never thought possible and could certainly not have brought about by our own strivings.

What is the heavenly Potter aiming at? What is the work that God has started and intends to bring to completion?

I have called it *wholeness*.

Paul expresses this in Colossians 1:28 when he says, 'That we may present everyone perfect in Christ.' In the RSV the word 'perfect' is translated 'mature'. It has in it the thought of completeness, maturity, a well-balanced, stable character, an increasingly integrated whole person. It means growing to be the unique persons God intended us to be. Above all, it means to become increasingly like the Lord Jesus. In 2 Corinthians 3:18 Paul writes, 'We . . . are being transformed into his likeness.' What a wonderful thing it is that the more we become truly ourselves, as God intends us to be, the more we shall be like him. It is only in him that we see perfectly expressed that image and likeness of God which has been so terribly spoiled in us through man's disobedience and choice to go his own way rather than God's way. The Lord Jesus is all God desires that a human being should be. In life and character he is God's pattern of wholeness.

We cannot separate the meaning of wholeness from the restoring of the relationships for which we were made: peace with God resulting in a living relationship with him; increasing peace within ourselves, and an increasing knowledge of how to live at peace with others. It is interesting that the Hebrew word translated as peace in the Old Testament includes the thought of wholeness.

Frequently in the Bible the process by which God is changing us is spoken of as growth. Sometimes we are pictured as trees or plants growing in height, beauty and fruitfulness. Sometimes we are pictured as buildings growing under the hand of the builder towards completeness. Sometimes we are thought of as babes or children growing towards adult maturity.

Growing is a quiet, gradual process which often takes place imperceptibly—the one who is growing not being conscious of his or her growth. There may be crises of growth when perhaps some obstacle to growth is removed and there seems to be rapid growth in a short time. Some truth, perhaps that of the power and work of the Holy Spirit, may come as a fresh revelation and cause a dramatic change. Or it may be that some particularly difficult or painful circumstance is walked through in a way which results in more rapid growth. But even if there are these crises it is the slow, steady growth which is the most healthy, and that continues throughout life.

The fact that growth is a quiet, gradual process and one which goes on throughout life does not mean that it is always without pain. If we think of ourselves as spoiled jars in the hands of the heavenly Potter, it is living, feeling human material which he is handling, not lifeless clay. There is much changing to be done, much moulding, much reshaping, many rough places to be made smooth. This will inevitably involve pain. If we use the picture of a plant or tree, there is need for the painful process of pruning as well as care that the life is nourished by water and minerals from the soil into which its roots go down. If we think of ourselves as children with a heavenly Father there is need for discipline; not the 'punishment' of a law court, but the training of a child. Training which involves teaching, correction and sometimes rebuke. About this the writer to the Hebrews says, 'No discipline seems pleasant at the time, but painful' (Heb 12:11).

The place of comfort regarding the painful side of growth is that we have seen the heart of the Potter, of the One who tends the plants, and of the Father in our Lord Jesus, and we know that the pain is not meaningless; he has a wonderful purpose in it; and behind and through it all is his love, his never-failing love.

Growing into wholeness does not take place in isolation. We need one another. It is through our human relationships as well as our relationship with God that we grow. Our own individual growth also contributes to the growth of the whole body of Christ, that is the company of all true Christians. Paul does not speak only of individual growth, he also speaks of the growth of the 'body of Christ', of which every Christian is a part. He tells us that the body is growing into maturity and likeness to

Christ. In Ephesians 4:11-16 he speaks of this. At the end of the passage he shows that it is through relationship with Christ and with one another that 'the whole body . . . grows and builds itself up in love, as each part does its work'. R. C. Lucas writes: 'Each Christian linked to Christ in this vital way, has some essential nourishment to give the whole body.'[1]

It is vitally important that we realize we each need nourishment from some body of Christians and, if we possibly can, should become part of some church or fellowship where we shall receive that nourishment. It is also important to realize that, however insignificant we feel, however little we feel we have to contribute, we each do have some essential nourishment to give. Without being conscious of it, our very presence supplies something of the life of the Lord Jesus to that body. I remember a minister speaking of the encouragement he got just from seeing certain people regularly in his congregation. I don't suppose they had any idea that they were supplying nourishment to their minister!

I have said that we need actively and wholeheartedly to co-operate with God in the growing process. Our part is *faith* which in the Bible has many different aspects and activities, but which is basically our response to God's initiative, and is made up of trust and obedience.

During the years that my husband was in medical practice in Kenya he occasionally needed to come to Britain for family reasons. It was on one of these occasions, when I was carrying on the practice, that a patient said to me, 'The matter with you doctors is that all you know comes from books, but I've got the pain!'

As I write about growing into wholeness I want to make it clear that I am not writing only through head knowledge that comes from books, even though the most important of these is the Bible. Each aspect of growth is one that has been and is being worked out in my own experience, often with its accompanying pain. It is my own experience and the experience of other Christians, as well as what I read in the Bible, that has led me to start by putting the emphasis where Paul puts it in 1 Corinthians 3:7, that it is God who makes things grow.

My Christian life started when I was at school. It extends over the years of being a medical student, many years of married life and the bringing up of our family in Kenya, East Africa, and then twenty years back in Britain. As I look back over the very varied experiences of the years, I remember that in the early days I longed to be a better Christian and a better witness, and often felt conscious of being a failure in my Christian life. There did not seem to be much growth. There was much longing for and striving after better things, and I used to seek for some crisis experience which would result in my becoming once and for all the kind of victorious Christian I thought I ought to be. I had many disappointments in this striving and seeking, then found that I was gradually giving it up and the emphasis was changing from what I needed to do and was striving to become, to what the Lord had committed himself to do in me. Of course I still had my struggles, as I still do, but at a deeper level than these there has been an increasing restfulness which I know comes from his life within me. It is that life which causes me to grow. It is a wonderful thing that this fact —that it is God who causes us to grow—was most vividly taught to me as a result of three and a half years of depression. For part of that time, I was incapable of consciously co-operating with the Lord in what he was doing; I could not even read my Bible or pray. Yet, at the end of that time, I came out more sure of my living relationship with him and more free emotionally than I had ever been before. I knew that he had been at work causing me to grow even through that dark time. This does not mean that since then I have felt no need to co-operate actively with the Lord. I think in fact it has been more active, but with much less strain about it.

In the following chapters, we shall think about some of the different aspects of growing into wholeness. Let us never forget that it is God who has committed himself to work in us and *he* who, by his Spirit within, gives us the ability to respond.

2

A RIGHT RELATIONSHIP
WITH GOD

The First Essential

Since God is the One who works in us so that we grow
into wholeness, the first essential is that we should be
in a right relationship with him. The image and likeness
of God was spoiled and distorted because man's relationship with God was broken. If the image is to be
restored, the relationship must be restored. This is in
keeping with our knowledge that the Lord Jesus is God's
perfect pattern of wholeness in a human being, for the
deepest reality in his personality was his relationship
with God.

A right relationship with God is that from which
everything else springs, and without it there can be no
growth into God's view of wholeness.

Jesus Christ is the way to a right relationship with God

In the first part of the letter to the Romans, Paul makes
it clear that we are all in the same condition; we have all
sinned, we are all alienated from God and all utterly
powerless to put things right. Then he comes to a glorious
'but now'.

'But now,' he says, 'God's way of putting people right
with himself has been revealed . . . by the free gift of

17

God's grace all are put right with him through Jesus Christ' (Rom 3:21, 24 GNB).

It is through the Lord Jesus, and only through him, that we are brought into a right relationship with God. He himself said, 'No-one comes to the Father except through me' (Jn 14:6). The cost to him of bridging the gulf between man and God was his great sacrifice on the cross when he took upon himself all our sin and guilt. When we receive the Lord Jesus into our lives, because we realize our need and our powerlessness to put things right, then he brings us into a right relationship with God. John puts it this way: 'To all who received him, to those who believed in his name, he gave the right to become children of God' (Jn 1:12).

This wonderful gift, the Lord Jesus Christ himself, through whom our relationship with God is restored, is over and over again spoken of as a *free* gift. We cannot earn this precious gift, we can never deserve it, we can only come with empty hands to receive what God has offered. Paul tells us that from our side a right relationship with God comes 'through faith in Jesus Christ' (Rom 3:22). We have seen that faith is our response to God's initiative. In this context God's initiative was the sending of his Son, the offering of the gift. Our response is the simple asking for the gift of the Lord Jesus Christ himself and then thanking God that he has given what he promised. A. Paget Wilkes, a missionary in Japan for years, described faith as: 'Forsaking **All** **I** **Take** **Him**.' 'Forsaking All' includes what the Bible means by repentance, which is basically a change of mind. Forsaking all my indifference to God's offer, all my self-righteousness; changing my mind from indifference to desire, from self-righteousness to an acknowledgement of sin and need. It means forsaking all my efforts to earn God's gift, to make myself worthy; changing my mind from endless striving to simple acceptance. 'I Take Him' is that act of accepting him, the Lord Jesus, as God's free gift, as the One who will bring me into that right relationship with God, which is the first step towards growth and wholeness.

While it is clear that it is only through Jesus Christ that we are brought into a right relationship with God, the ways in which people come to know him vary greatly. I have heard boys and girls, men and women, young and old, from various countries and with differing backgrounds, tell of how they came to know the Lord Jesus and all their stories have been different.

I myself remember the day when as a teenager, and desperately wanting to know that I was a child of God, I found the words in John 6:37 (AV): 'Him that cometh to me I will in no wise cast out.' I told him I knew he had died for me, I wanted to know my sins were forgiven and that I was a true Christian. I was coming to him as best I knew how and was going to hold on to the promise that he would not cast me out but would receive me. It wasn't many days after that when the quiet certainty came into my heart that he had received me. I know others who have found that same verse to be the door into a relationship with God.

Another verse which has helped many to find the way is Revelation 3:20 (AV): 'Behold, I stand at the door, and knock: if any man hear my voice, and open the door, I will come in.' These, knowing their need of him, have invited the Lord Jesus to come into their lives and to take possession of them.

I know others who don't remember a specific day as I do, but have told me that over a period of time there was a dawning realization of their need and a growing certainty that Jesus Christ is alive and had become their Saviour and Friend. One of these said, 'I don't remember a particular day when I came to God through Christ, I only know that now I can say that I am his.'

Others, brought up with a knowledge of the Christian faith, do not remember a time when they did not have a relationship with the Lord Jesus. That which started when they were children has grown and developed over the years.

Years ago a married woman, who until recently had had no knowledge of the Christian faith, came to see me. She said she wanted to be a true Christian. She had asked the Lord Jesus to come into her life, to forgive her sins and to receive her into the family of God, but she was not sure whether she had the right to say that she was a child of God because she knew so little about these things. After talking for a while she said, 'One thing I do know is that I am no longer comfortable with people I used to be comfortable with, and I *am* comfortable with people I used not to be comfortable with.' I thought that was delightful! I told her I believed that John would have said that was a sign of being one of God's children. In 1 John 3:14 he says, 'We know that we have passed from death to life, because we love our brothers.' She was very comforted and re-assured by this.

Two precious gifts

When we receive the Lord Jesus Christ, he gives us two most precious gifts which Peter spoke of at the end of his sermon on the day of Pentecost (Acts 2:38). The first of these is *the forgiveness of sin*. Apart from that gift there could be no right relationship with God. We have broken God's law, we have gone our own way instead of his way, there is a long list of convictions against us; we need his forgiveness for these. We have robbed God of his rightful place in our lives, of the love and worship we owe him. We have run up a long list of debts which we

are quite unable to pay; we need his forgiveness for
these. We have hurt and wounded our Maker by our
indifference to him and by the spoiling of his property;
we need forgiveness for this. The Lord Jesus brings us a
King's pardon—full and free forgiveness. Not only are
we forgiven, we are also made clean. Clean from all our
guilt, our soiling, our pollution. We can stand before him
forgiven and with a sense of having been washed, of
being clean. What a gift!

The second gift is that of *the Holy Spirit*. Apart from
this gift there could be no growth, no change in us. He is
the Spirit of life; he brings into our personalities the very
life of God, the life of the Lord Jesus. It is this life that is
the power and energy which brings about growth.

The Holy Spirit is also what Paul calls '*the Spirit of
sonship*' (Rom 8:15). It is he who assures us that we are
children of God and causes us to call God our Father. In
this he is already making us like Jesus who so repeatedly
spoke of God as 'my Father'. It is he who gives us that
knowledge of belonging to our Father and to his family.
We no longer belong in the law court with its atmosphere
of accusation and condemnation. We have been for ever
lifted out of that and received into the Father's house.
Sharing his life, we are free to grow up into his likeness
as his sons and daughters.

He is also '*the Spirit of truth*' who teaches us and
guides us into all truth (Jn 16:13). There is no more
important truth into which he will guide us than that of
the character of our Father. There are many who judge
the character of the heavenly Father by the grossly distorted picture of fatherhood which they have received
from their earthly fathers. And the character of the best
of earthly fathers is only a faint shadow of the character
of our Father in heaven. We need to judge the standard
of earthly fatherhood by the heavenly, not the heavenly

by the earthly. Patiently, the Holy Spirit corrects our thinking so that, increasingly, we grow more like the Lord Jesus in our knowledge of the true character of the Father. He said, 'Anyone who has seen me has seen the Father' (Jn 14:9). Look at Jesus and we know what the Father is like. Listen to his teaching as he taught about his Father. The Father is One who knows us, who cares about us, who gives to us and, above all, whose arms are open to receive us as the father received his prodigal son in the parable told in Luke 15.

In my own life I have found that it is not enough just to know that I have received these two gifts. I need to seek to live in daily realization of what it means to be a forgiven person, and in active expectation of the work of the Holy Spirit in my life.

A right relationship with God is one which sets us free

Jesus said, 'If the Son sets you free, you will be free indeed' (Jn 8:36). R. C. Lucas writes: 'It is inconceivable that God should forgive the past, and then send us back incapable of living a new life. Pardon without deliverance would be a mockery. . . .'[2]

It is these two gifts, forgiveness and the Holy Spirit linked together, which set us free. When people think that to become a Christian would take away their freedom, they are accepting one of Satan's greatest lies. There can be no real freedom apart from a right relationship with our Maker.

When Jesus said, 'If the Son sets you free, you will be free indeed' (Jn 8:36), he was speaking about slavery to *sin*. 'Everyone who sins is a slave to sin' (Jn 8:34). If we are to grasp the miracle of his setting us free, we need the Spirit of truth to give us a right concept of sin. Notice that the Lord Jesus did not say 'a slave to sins', he said 'a slave to *sin*'. Sins are like symptoms, *sin* is the disease.

William Temple says: 'We try to cure our symptoms—our habits of lying, cheating, or resentment, or envy, or contempt, or impurity—but we leave the disease alone. But the disease is that we are self-centred, not God-centred. . . .'[3]

The enormity of sin in all of us is that the central place which God who made us and loves us should have, has been usurped in our personalities by 'me'. Self-centredness, which is the essence of sin, is the most destructive force in the universe, and behind that force is Satan, who is always out to destroy. It frequently shows itself in ways other than what we call great sins or flagrant sins. It is only as the Holy Spirit begins to show us our own particular manifestations of self-centredness that we realize how it robs us of true freedom, and that we cry to God for deliverance. When we receive the Lord Jesus and he enters our lives, he brings God back into his rightful place at the centre of our personalities. He begins to break the domination and destructiveness of our self-centredness. Freed from this slavery, we begin to experience 'a freedom that is unafraid to be in Christ, the person God made us'.[4] We begin to be able to say to the Lord, 'Not what I will, but what you will' (Mk 14:36).

A relationship with God is a relationship of love

In Romans 5:1 Paul speaks of being in a right relationship with God through Jesus Christ, and in verse 5 he says, 'God has poured out his love into our hearts by the Holy Spirit, whom he has given us.' Later, he brings to a climax his wonderful eighth chapter with the words:

> I am convinced that neither death nor life, neither angels nor demons, neither the present nor the future, nor any

powers, neither height nor depth, nor anything else in all creation, will be able to separate us from the love of God that is in Christ Jesus our Lord (Rom 8:38-39).

When Paul said, 'Love builds up' (1 Cor 8:1), he was speaking of God's love expressed in relationships in the family of God. The Holy Spirit may use human channels for the pouring of God's love into our hearts. Whether direct from God in our relationship with him or through fellow Christians, it is love that causes us to grow. It is said that plants grow better if they are loved. Watch the jar in the potter's hands grow into a thing of beauty and you will know that he loves the picture of the finished product which he has in his mind, and he loves the material he is working with. Love, shown in early relationships, is the greatest contribution towards a child growing up into emotional stability. Where there is absence of love or where the flow of love is blocked or hindered in relationships, growth is limited or slowed down.

If love contributes to plant growth, to the growth of a work of art, and is a vital factor in the growth of a child, how much more is it the most vital factor in our growth into that wholeness which God desires? His love, in all its aspects, is the nourishment needed for growth and it is also the mighty power by which hindrances to its flow in our relationships are swept away.

Let us look at some aspects of the wonderful love which is poured into our hearts by the Holy Spirit and from which nothing can separate us when we have been brought into a right relationship with God.

God's love is measureless

The Lord Jesus said, 'As the Father has loved me, so have I loved you' (Jn 15:9); and later he prayed to his

Father: 'That the love you have for me may be in them' (Jn 17:26). How can we measure the love of the Father for his Son? It is breathtaking to begin to realize that it is that love which is brought to us through Jesus when he brings us into a right relationship with the Father. He links us up with a measureless ocean of love. In the light of this, how can we measure our worth to God? We are infinitely precious, his treasured possession. Unworthy, totally unworthy, but of infinite worth.

God's love is unconditional

W. E. Sangster describes this aspect of God's love in glowing terms:

> They know themselves loved *for* nothing: just for themselves . . . He is not loving them *if* they will do this, or *if* they will do that. He loves them for themselves alone. Nothing in them created that love and nothing in them can drive it away. It is love without condition and it is love without end.[5]

It is this unconditional love that assures us that he accepts us just as we are, and which does much to drive away our deep fear of rejection. It is an acceptance which provides us with a security which makes change and growth possible. Remember that all God's gifts are free gifts. His love comes to us as a free gift. If it depends on us reaching some standard, whatever that standard may be; if we fear that we shall lose it if we fail to reach that standard, then we are thinking in terms of an exchange, not a gift. The more value we set on the gift, the more we will reject any idea of an exchange.

God's love is steadfast

This word, used many times in the Old Testament (RSV), can be described well by the first line of George Matheson's hymn 'O Love, that wilt not let me go'.

There may be times in our lives when we feel that we have lost our hold of him. At these times we know that if our relationship with him depended on our hold of him, we would be lost. But, thank God, he never loses hold of us! My own experience is that it is the very times when I have felt that I have lost my hold of him, that have resulted in the deepest assurance that he had not lost his hold of me. It is a love that never ends. Through Jeremiah God said, 'I have loved you with an everlasting love' (Jer 31:3). It is a love that was displayed in the Lord Jesus when John wrote of him, 'He had always loved those in the world who were his own, and he loved them to the very end' (Jn 13:1 GNB). It is a love that is utterly dependable, utterly faithful, never changing however much we may change. A love that causes us to sing:

> Great is thy faithfulness, O God my Father,
> There is no shadow of turning with thee.
> Thou changest not, thy compassions they fail not.
> As thou hast been, thou forever wilt be.
>
> *T.O. Chisholm*

God's love is understanding

'You know me,' said the psalmist (Ps 139:1). 'Thou knowest me through and through' (Ps 139:14 NEB).

Understanding is a very precious aspect of human love. The more we feel understood, the more we feel loved. But no human being can understand us perfectly. To say that I can read someone like a book (which I remember someone saying about me when I was a child!), is nonsense. I have probably got no further than the introduction! God alone understands us perfectly. Because the Lord Jesus lives in us by his Spirit, he has an inner knowledge of us which no one else has. It is because he knows and understands us perfectly that he is able to do a healing work within us (see Isaiah 57:18). He can heal the deep wounds. He can straighten out the twists in our personalities. He knows how to break the inner chains that bind us.

God's love is purifying

There is nothing soft or weak about God's love. There is something relentless about it. It is set relentlessly against everything that destroys and mars our personalities. How could he really love us if this were not so? Love is sometimes likened in the Bible to fire: 'It burns like blazing fire' (Song 8:6). That fire does not destroy God's children, it purifies them, purging out that which is unlike himself. This cannot be other than a painful process, but even in the purifying he is wonderfully tender and compassionate.

When God's people had been through a terrible purifying experience Jeremiah said, 'Though he brings grief, he will show compassion, so great is his unfailing love. For he does not willingly bring affliction or grief to the children of men' (Lam 3:32-33).

There is a lot of purifying to be done if we are to be made like Jesus. When we feel the pain of it let us remember that whatever the outward circumstances the deepest fact is God's *love*. It is God's purifying love which is the compelling power in freeing us from the rule of self-centredness in our lives. Paul said, 'For Christ's love compels us, because we are convinced that one died for all, and therefore all died. And he died for all, that those who live should no longer live for themselves but for him who died for them and was raised again' (2 Cor 5:14-15). It is his love which will compel us to seek to choose his way rather than our way in the practical details of daily living.

Rooted and established in love

In his great prayer recorded in Ephesians 3:14-21, Paul asked that the Christians at Ephesus might be rooted and established in love. The picture which this suggests is that of a tree with its roots going deep down into the soil, drawing from that soil all the rich nourishment needed to cause it to grow and to become stable and strong. The deeper our roots go down into the love of God, the more we shall find the nourishment that is needed for our growth. Paul acknowledges in this prayer that this is the work of the Holy Spirit, making real the presence of Christ living in us. He also speaks of grasping the greatness of Christ's love, which is the love of God, so that we begin to know in experience that love which goes far beyond all knowledge.

The word 'grasp' could be translated 'take hold of'. The way to get the roots of our personalities established in any truth is to keep taking hold of that truth until at last the time comes when that truth takes hold of us. Then we begin to say, 'Oh, I see!' and to experience the power of the truth. We can pray that the Holy Spirit will give us the power so to take hold of the truth of God's love that it will really take hold of us. Only then will we begin to know that love as a daily experience in a way which will inwardly change us and give us an ever-deepening trust in our Father. Only as the reality of God's love takes hold of us will it hold us firm and stable in the midst of the storms of life.

Our response to God's initiative in giving us this immeasurable gift of his love in the Lord Jesus, could well be to make Paul's prayer our prayer. We can ask that the Lord Jesus will enable us constantly to feed on different aspects of his love.

We can ask that he will give us the power to affirm the

truth of his love even in the times when our feelings will be crying out against it. There may be times when doubts concerning God's love and our relationship with him become overwhelming. Our hearts may cry out, 'I don't *feel* he loves me; I don't *feel* he understands me; I cannot believe that I am precious to him.' At those times it is a triumph of faith to be able to say, 'I know that it is my feelings that are telling lies; the truth is that he loves me, even *me*.' The deeper we are rooted in the love of God the more we spontaneously respond in love and trust to our Father.

We can spend time at the cross, which is the place above all others, where we see the love of God in Jesus Christ. The more we are rooted in his love, the more we shall be open to giving and receiving love in our human relationships. In this, more than in any other way, we shall be contributing to the growth of the body of Christ. Writing of that body, Paul says it 'grows and builds itself up in love, as each part does its work' (Eph 4:16).

3

CONTINUED FELLOWSHIP
WITH GOD

The Forgiving Love of God

I am a forgiven person

We have seen that the first essential for growth is to be
brought into a right relationship with God. Having been
brought into that right relationship, there is nothing more
important than that we should continue in unclouded
fellowship with God. If this is to be our experience, we
need constantly to enjoy *the forgiving love of God*.

In my own personal experience and in years of coun-
selling and speaking, I have come to a conviction that
there is nothing more important for growth than that
Christians should live in the enjoyment of the fullness
and ongoing nature of God's forgiveness. As Christians,
we know that there was nothing in us which deserved or
could ever earn the right to a loving relationship with
God. It came about only and wholly through the free gift
of his forgiveness. We have no question about that being
the condition on which we became his children. While
we acknowledge with no difficulty that that is true, we
very easily slip into an attitude of thinking and feeling
that once we are Christians God's conditions for our
continuing to enjoy loving fellowship with him and all his
blessings are different. We probably would not say that,

but we reveal it when we say, 'I don't feel I'm worthy', 'I don't think I deserve', 'I don't feel I can expect God to bless', 'I'm not good enough', 'I've got to get this put right before I can come freely to him', 'I don't think I have enough faith', and so on, as though faith was money with which to buy God's gifts, rather than our response to his offer of a *free* gift.

The truth is that first to last our unclouded fellowship and friendship with him depends, not on our worthiness or goodness or success or anything else, but only and wholly on our being forgiven people. Paul said, 'Just as you received . . . continue to live' (Col 2:6). God received us into his life of friendship in spite of our total unworthiness. We are to live as those who have given up every effort to make ourselves worthy.

Forgiveness is not just a series of separate gifts of forgiveness for which we ask because we are conscious we have sinned, but like a great ocean in which we swim; or, to change the picture, *the* condition on which we as little children have free and constant access to a loving Father. For this reason, I want us to look at the subject more closely, with the prayer that we will get a greater vision of the length, breadth, height and depth of the forgiving love of God.

1. *The Lord Jesus has done all that is necessary for our full forgiveness*

In Hebrews 9:26 we read, 'He has appeared once for all . . . to do away with sin by the sacrifice of himself.' The death of the Lord Jesus on the cross was a 'once for all' sacrifice. It need not be repeated; it cannot be repeated. We need add nothing. We can only come and continue to come the way of forgiveness with empty hands and, as the hymn-writer says, 'Just as I am.'

We have strange ways of trying to add to that sacrifice;

ways of punishing ourselves, perhaps by withdrawing
from the Father's presence and putting ourselves under a
little penal servitude before we feel we can go freely
back to him. Sometimes we feel we need to buy his
forgiveness (though we would never admit it), with a
certain amount of sorrow. I have heard some people say,
'I don't think I was sorry enough,' and my reply has
always been, 'How sorry do you feel you've got to be to
buy your forgiveness?' No! The sacrifice has been made,
the price has been paid. Don't let us minimize it by
trying to add to it.

Not only has Jesus done all that is necessary for our
full forgiveness but, in his death on the cross, he has
shown us in an unmistakable way the forgiving heart of
God. He said, 'Anyone who has seen me has seen the
Father' (Jn 14:9). We need have no question as regards
the forgiving heart of the Father, his willingness to forgive,
his longing to forgive. We need have no question as
regards the completeness and finality of what Jesus has
done to make possible our forgiveness.

2. *The sacrifice of the Lord Jesus means forgiveness for all that the Bible calls sin*

Sin in the Bible includes more than we sometimes think
of as sin, which means that forgiveness covers more than
we tend to realize.

Sin in the Bible includes *all known sin*, *all acts of sin*.
John writes: 'If we confess our sins, he is faithful and just
and will forgive us our sins' (1 Jn 1:9). If I know I have
sinned or been disobedient, the moment I confess, which
means acknowledging it to God, I am forgiven and
fellowship is restored. At that moment I can run as a
little child without any restriction into the presence of
the Father. He will show me whether or not I need to
confess to any human being. The important thing is that

I should first confess to him and know his forgiveness.

Another aspect of sin in the Bible is *error*. Sin includes errors, mistakes and failures. Sometimes our errors, our mistakes, our failures (none of which were deliberate or intentional) cloud our fellowship with guilty feelings more than the definite, known acts of sin which we can confess and for which we receive forgiveness. It is these that so easily lead to feelings of unworthiness and self-condemnation, instead of to accepting forgiveness. We have not really grasped that God's forgiveness includes these. And yet many, many of these must be unconscious to us, yet very clear to God. No wonder the Psalmist said, 'Who can discern his errors? Forgive my hidden faults' (Ps 19:12). I praise God that he does not pull us up for every error, every mistake, every failure. If he did, he would be at it all day long! What a lot there is to forgive.

Yet another meaning of sin is *missing the mark*. Paul calls it falling short of the glory of God (Rom 3:23). What is the mark we miss? What is the standard we fall short of? It is perfect likeness to the Lord Jesus Christ, who shows us in his life and character what God intended man to be. When I think of that and then of my own life and character I realize I am falling short or missing the mark all the time, and will do until I get to heaven and am perfectly like the Lord Jesus. Realizing this, as we all must, how is it that God ever continues to have fellowship with us? Only because the sacrifice of the Lord Jesus means forgiveness for all my falling short. This is more to do with what I *am* than with what I *do*. God forgives you for what you are, as well as for what you do. It is in thinking of us like that that H. R. Mackintosh writes: 'To the Saint [i.e. the Christian] it is a daily discovery that God does not cast him out. Christian as he is, he remains a sinner.'[6]

It is very possible for us to spend a lot of time moaning

inside ourselves about what we are, rather than rejoicing in that forgiveness which makes possible, in spite of all we are, the unspoiled friendship and fellowship with the Lord, through which we shall inevitably become more like him.

3. *The fullness of his forgiveness*

The Bible gives us several pictures to help us grasp the fullness of God's forgiveness. 'As far as the east is from the west', 'I've swept away your offences', 'Into the depths of the sea', 'You have put all my sins behind your back'. One of the most wonderful statements is in Hebrews 8:12, 'I will forgive their wickedness, and will remember their sins no more.' No more! God actually has the power to put out of his memory the sins he has forgiven. This cannot mean less than that he never brings up against us past sin that he has forgiven. The forgiven sin of yesterday need never cloud today's fellowship. When we feel ashamed to ask his forgiveness again for some sin, perhaps some habit which we consider to be sinful that keeps getting us down, someone has suggested that God says, 'What do you mean *again*?' For there is no past score against us! It is only as we accept his repeated forgiveness that we shall maintain that closeness to him which is the one hope of overcoming the sin, of breaking the habit, for *he alone* can set us free. 'But,' someone says, 'don't I have to repent, and doesn't that mean that I commit myself not to do the thing again?' Yes, you do have to repent, but repentance does not mean such a commitment. The Lord knows and we know (if we are aware of our own frailty), that we cannot give that assurance. Repentance is basically a change of mind, a change of direction. It means a change from thinking a thing is not wrong to thinking it is wrong; and a change of direction from looking anywhere else, to one of looking only and wholly to him for the forgiveness and power to set free which he alone can give. It includes an intention to seek his way of freedom.

4. *God takes up the results of sin he has forgiven*

It is a mistake to think that forgiveness does away with all the consequences of our sins, or that if we are suffering from the consequences it means we are not forgiven. When sin is forgiven, the consequences become the discipline of a loving Father who is present with us in the discipline, not hiding his face from us. I know someone who remembers vividly what happened when, as a child, she was away with her family on holiday. She tells how a visit to a beautiful sea-water swimming pool was one of the highlights of each day. One morning she complained of a slight sore throat, but pleaded with her mother to allow her to go to the pool with her brother. With the promise (rather unrealistically accepted by Mother!) that she would not spend more than twenty minutes in the water and that she would ask the attendant to say when the time was up, her mother sent them off. After a very long time they returned. It was very obvious that any promise had been thrown to the winds and that she had got thoroughly chilled. That night she had a raging sore throat and high temperature. The thing that remains in her memory and has spoken to her about the forgiving heart of God, is that her mother stayed with her, and cared for her just as lovingly as if she had not been disobedient. The consequences were not removed (we hope they taught her a lesson!), but the forgiving heart of the mother and her active forgiveness were shown in her loving desire to help the child to bear the suffering which resulted from her disobedience.

J. H. Jowett, writing about 'Thou hast beset me behind' (Ps 139:5), says:

He defends me from the hostility of my own past . . . consequences are not annihilated; their operations are changed. They are transformed from destructives into constructives. The sword becomes a plough-share . . . the sins of yesterday no longer send their poisoned swords into my life.[7]

What about the results in the lives of others of our sins, mistakes and failures? There must be many times when our hearts cry out, 'It's wonderful to know that I am forgiven, but what about the results? I've wronged, I've harmed my friends, my relatives, my neighbours, my children; has the Lord got anything to say to me about that?' There are some things we can put right and if we can we must. If we have wronged the Inland Revenue by a dishonest filling in of tax returns, we can and must put that right. Sadly, there are many occasions when we have wronged or harmed people and it is beyond our power to put it right. The Bible shows us that in the sacrifice of the Lord Jesus there is not only forgiveness, there is the putting right of wrong. Since one of the Old Testament sacrifices provided for forgiveness and for the putting right of wrong done, of harm inflicted (Lev 5:14–6:7), how much more does that perfect sacrifice of the Lord Jesus!

Someone writing on Psalm 23:6 (AV) says, '"Surely goodness and mercy shall follow me" . . . the Calvary goodness and mercy clears up behind us as well as clears a way before us . . . to heal the wounds which we have inflicted, to redress the wrongs which we have committed, to neutralize the consequences of our folly and ignorance and sin.'[8]

We get another glimpse of this truth in Isaiah 52:12, which ends with these words: 'The Lord will go before you, the God of Israel will be your rearguard.' One of my brothers has for years held Boys' Camps under canvas every summer. An advance guard goes ahead and puts up the tents and gets everything ready. Then the boys come and all is life and activity for several weeks. At the end, a small number of men and older boys stays behind to form what they call the rear guard. The job of the rear guard is to clear up the mess the boys have left behind!

God is our rear guard who not only protects us from Satan's accusations about the past, but actually clears up the mess we leave behind. In wonderful ways, the Lord Jesus does take into his pierced hands the results of our sins and failures. So when our hearts are torn, we can go to the cross and, claiming all that the Lord Jesus made possible by his sacrifice, we can ask God somehow, sometime, to make up to others for the harm or wrong we have done to them.

I have been asked whether speaking like this about the fullness of God's forgiveness and the results of God's forgiveness would encourage people to take a light view of sin. Paul had a similar question asked him when he had written of God's grace: 'Shall we go on sinning, so that grace may increase?' My answer would be the same as his: 'By no means!' (Rom 6:1). We have seen that to live in the enjoyment of God's full and ongoing forgiveness for all our sins, errors, mistakes, failures and for all our falling short, means to live in unclouded fellowship and friendship with him. How can fellowship and friendship with a *holy* God result in anything other than to give us a greater hatred of sin in all its forms? How can it result in anything other than growth in likeness to Jesus, his 'holy servant'? (Acts 4:27). How can it result in anything other than the increasing control of his *Holy* Spirit? Besides, I have never known any to be exercised over this question except those who take a very serious view of sin and its results.

Let us never forget that forgiveness is costly, both to give and to receive. Go again to the cross to see the infinite cost of our forgiveness. Then what is the cost, not of earning or deserving, but of receiving? Paul tells us in Philippians 3. It cost him the loss of every shred of self-righteousness. If we are to receive God's forgiveness over and over again and live in the enjoyment of his continuing forgiveness all through our Christian lives, it will cost us the loss of every shred of self-righteousness. And that is another reason why the ongoing experience of forgiveness will result in growth! All this means that if I keep short accounts with the Lord concerning the sin I know, then no shadow from the past, nor my consciousness of my continuing unworthiness, need cloud my fellowship with him in the present. I can bask in the sunshine of his forgiveness, knowing that he does indeed keep on cleansing me from *all* sin (see 1 John 1:7).

Am I a forgiving person?

Forgiving others

As we learn more of the greatness and permanent nature of our forgiveness, we shall inevitably grow more like the Lord Jesus in our capacity to be forgiving people. Since it is through our human relationships as well as in our relationship with God that we grow, the human channels for life and love must be kept open, and destructive factors removed. An unforgiving spirit, so often taking the form of resentment, is a very destructive factor. However justified we may feel our resentment to be, it still has a destructive effect if we nurse or feed it. It is destructive within ourselves. It does not build us up and make us more mature, more Christ-like people. It is like a festering wound. In fact, past wounds never heal while they are poisoned by resentment. It is also destructive in relationships. How tragic it is when a widening gulf of resentment divides those who should be in close relationship: the married couple, the parent and son or daughter, the friends, the fellow-Christians. If we nurse resentment, the whole atmosphere is destructive and it certainly does not contribute to the growth of others.

One of the most solemn stories in the Bible about the end result of an unforgiving spirit is the story of the beheading of John the Baptist. Herod had made that foolish promise to Herodias' daughter that he would give her whatever she asked. Prompted by Herodias, she asked for John the Baptist's head, and when it was given to her she brought it to her mother. Where did that story start? Mark tells us that it started in Herodias' heart; she nursed a grudge against John (Mk 6:19). She would not forgive him for what he had said about the unlawfulness of their marriage. How terrible to think that the seed which grew to the harvest of murder was just a grudge. I wonder what Herodias really felt when she was presented with that head! Should we not look very seriously at the seed when we find it in our own hearts?

The Lord Jesus taught that an unforgiving spirit is a hindrance to fellowship with himself. He said, 'For if you forgive men when they sin against you, your heavenly Father will also forgive you. But if you do not forgive men their sins, your Father will not forgive your sins' (Mt 6:14-15).

The Lord Jesus was not speaking about a condition for entering his kingdom. He was speaking to his disciples about conditions for fellowship in his kingdom. It applies to those who are Christians and can call God their Father. What he is saying, in effect, is that if we will not forgive others, we shall find that we are out of fellowship with him. On several occasions the Lord Jesus taught that an unforgiving spirit is a hindrance to prayer. On one of these occasions he said, 'When you stand praying, if you hold anything against anyone, forgive him' (Mk 11:25). Anything against anyone! The Amplified Version says,

'Let it drop—leave it, let it go.' Prayer is coming to God with empty hands to receive. It is impossible to receive if I am holding on to things which I will not forgive in others. I must let them drop.

God has given us himself as an example of how we are to forgive one another. Paul says, 'Forgiving each other, just as in Christ God forgave you' (Eph 4:32). That is only possible because the Lord Jesus does live in us. It is his forgiving love continuously working in and through our human hearts that makes it in any way possible for us to forgive as we have been forgiven.

I want to think about a forgiving spirit rather than the mechanics of forgiveness. Behind the forgiveness of God is the forgiving love of his heart. So it is with us. If our hearts are taken over by the forgiving love of Jesus we shall be able, in any particular instance, to find the way of forgiveness, which will be different in different situations. For instance, if we have been sinned against and fellowship has been broken, it can only be restored fully if there is confession and a desire for reconciliation. If one partner in a marriage commits adultery, there can only be forgiveness, in the sense of restoration of fellowship, on the grounds of confession and repentance. In this and similar situations, there can be a forgiving spirit, which means the open door of willingness to forgive the moment the conditions are fulfilled. It also means getting rid of resentment, bitterness and the desire to punish. It does not mean the end of pain, but it may mean the willingness to give up the desire that the other person shall know the extent of the pain caused!

A forgiving spirit will find the way to let drop the many errors, mistakes and shortcomings of others which so often build up resentment in close relationships. It is possible for little things to build up such resentment between two people that they reach the point of not

41

speaking to one another. This does in fact all too frequently happen in marriages, church fellowships and in friendships.

If you have a forgiving spirit, the Lord will show you whether you need to talk to the other person about the thing you have resented or whether you should just let it drop. The vital thing is that we should not let resentment grow by nursing or feeding it. Bring it quickly up into the light of God's presence, talk to him about it and then it will never eat its way into your personality—he will handle it.

A question that is often asked is whether it is possible to put out of our memory that which we have forgiven, in the way that God does. Yes, I believe it is possible for *God* to take right out of our memories the things that we have forgiven. But I think this often takes a long time. In actual practice, I believe it begins by refusing to bring up against others the things we say we have forgiven. Paul says, 'Love . . . keeps no record of wrongs' (1 Cor 13:5).

At the end of a meeting, during which a preacher had spoken on this subject, a woman went away under deep conviction. The next day, when people were being asked to say ways in which they had been blessed, she said, 'Last night when I got home, I asked the Lord to help me to throw away my "despisory".' She went on to say that she had realized she kept at the back of her mind what was like a card index system of all the things that people had done against her and for which she had despised them. Whenever one of these people did anything that hurt her, she pulled out the card belonging to that person, and brought to mind all their previous offences. At that meeting the Lord had shown her that if she wanted to know the fullness of his forgiveness, that card index had to be thrown away. Persisting faithfully in this attitude is the pathway towards forgetting.

I do not know of any more moving and clear description of the struggle to forgive in someone greatly sinned against, than that told by Rita Nightingale in her book, *Freed For Life*. She became a Christian while in a prison in Thailand on a false charge of smuggling heroin. She writes honestly of her feelings of not wanting to forgive and of the encouragement given to her by two Christian friends to be open with the Lord about all her feelings of bitterness. Towards the end of the chapter describing this she says:

> It was a slow and painful progression. Each person had to be prayed over, agonised over, and forgiven. When I thought I had really forgiven somebody, I would find myself resenting them two or three days later, and have to forgive them all over again.
>
> It was only as I looked back, as the days became weeks and the weeks months, that I saw that my attitudes were changing. I was learning how to forgive.[9]

If we want to grow more like the Lord Jesus in his forgiving love, there is no better way than to think of how much we have been forgiven. Let us think about it: all known sin, all errors and mistakes, all the perpetual falling short of God's standard. All that we know about ourselves and all that God knows and that we don't. Let us add it up and then, alongside, let us assess how much we are being asked to forgive. I find that is the most likely exercise to melt my heart. If we will not forgive, it means that we have never really appreciated the fullness of our own forgiveness.

Forgiving myself

What do people mean when they say, 'I know God has forgiven me but I can't forgive myself'? What do *you* mean if you are one of those who says it? If you are not, can you understand those who do say it (sometimes with tears running down their faces) and can you help them? It is worth trying to understand because remorse, which is probably the right word to use, hinders our growth. Remorse is sure to cloud our fellowship with God and no one who is full of remorse is at peace within. Let me say what I mean when I say, 'I cannot forgive myself.' I mean that although I know God has forgiven me I still feel guilty; I cannot let the matter drop, it keeps coming back and worrying me or even tormenting me. Sometimes it makes me angry with myself and causes me to keep on punishing myself. I find it difficult to face the fact that it was I who did whatever it was, that I am that kind of person. It doesn't just make me feel unworthy, it tends to make me feel worth-less. The past does not rest as a forgiven past but is at any moment liable to spring up and intrude into the present.

Elizabeth Goudge, in her autobiography *Joy of the Snow*, expresses something of the effect of remorse and the necessity to forgive ourselves:

> There is no one harder to forgive than oneself, it can take years. Nevertheless we know inside ourselves that it must be done, for remorse is a sin which rots away the very vitals of the soul. And we know well the price of a soul to God.[10]

Do you 'know well the price of a soul to God'? The price he was willing to pay for your soul and for my soul was the Lord Jesus Christ, his only Son. We should certainly not 'let rot' that for which he paid such a price. Certainly, remorse as well as resentment prevents old wounds from healing.

How then can we get rid of remorse and learn to forgive ourselves?

The first step is to face the fact that it is *wrong* not to forgive ourselves. That is not always easy! Some people feel they ought not to forgive themselves; they have been so bad they ought to continue to feel guilty and be punished. In some there is a strange kind of self-pity which is hard to let go of. If we think of how destructive remorse is; if we think of the fact that it hinders fellowship with the Lord; if we realize that it lays us open to Satan's accusations, we must acknowledge that it is wrong. Most of all, since we know that GOD has forgiven us, are we not putting ourselves above God if we do not forgive ourselves?

Having accepted that it is wrong not to forgive ourselves, then we must come to the Lord and ask him to change our experience of the past about which we have so much remorse. He alone can do this. We can ask him to show us ways in which we are punishing ourselves and to help us to stop doing it. We can ask him to handle our feelings about ourselves. We can ask him to make it possible for us to affirm that however unworthy we may be, this particular sin or failure does not make us more unworthy than we already were! And *nothing* can alter our infinite worth to him; for that does not depend on what we do or don't do, but on the fact that he created us and that we are his precious children.

Once again, it is at the cross that we are most helped to see afresh the price he paid for our forgiveness and to open our hearts to his forgiving love in a way which will make it possible to forgive ourselves.

Sometimes it is difficult to know whether or not we have forgiven ourselves, especially when there is still pain or sorrow about some past event. Certainly, pain and sorrow do not necessarily mean that we have not forgiven ourselves. Getting rid of remorse does not necessarily mean losing all the pain and sorrow, but it does mean that they will lose their festering and paralysing power. The pain or sorrow will be that of a healing wound rather than of a festering one. It will not cause us to be constantly turned in on ourselves, but will be an incentive towards closer fellowship with the Lord and concern for others.

Paul had a tremendous lot for which to forgive himself. When writing to Timothy he said:

> I thank Christ Jesus our Lord, who has given me strength, that he considered me faithful, appointing me to his service. Even though I was once a blasphemer and a persecutor and a violent man . . . Christ Jesus came into the world to save sinners—of whom I am the worst. But for that very reason I was shown mercy so that in me, the worst of sinners, Christ Jesus might display his unlimited patience (1 Tim 1:12-16).

I cannot believe that Paul ever lost the pain and sorrow of what he had done in being the cause of the imprisonment and death of many Christians. What we do know is that the mercy, patience and forgiveness of God were uppermost in his mind, not his past sins. If he had been eaten up with remorse and unable to forgive himself, his past sins would have been uppermost and he would have been hindered in his fellowship with the Lord and in his service for the Lord.

Forgiven and forgiving

These two are bound closely together. The more we live in the enjoyment of the wonder and reality of God's forgiving love and his continuous forgiveness, the more will we become forgiving people. The more our hearts are open to his forgiving love, the more our relationships will contribute to our own growth and that of others, because they are free from the destructive factors of guilt, resentment and remorse.

4

CHRISTIAN CONTENTMENT

An Atmosphere that Promotes Growth

The attractive nature of contentment

I cannot think of any attitude of mind more encouraging
to growth than contentment. It is interesting to see that
the more contented we are at any stage of life, the easier
it is to develop and adapt to the next stage. The child
who is contented at home is more likely to adapt easily to
school; the boy or girl who is contented at school is more
likely to adapt easily to early adult life. Sadly, we sometimes see the reverse in old age—a pathetically discontented person clinging most fiercely to life.

Contentment is also such an attractive quality. I remember how, when I was a girl at school, the deep
contentment which I saw in a Christian woman created
in me a longing to find her secret. I know that this played
a vital part in bringing me to a knowledge of the Lord
Jesus. Amy Carmichael writes, 'How good if by His
blessed enabling we should daily so receive his peace
that others should . . . only find when they come the gift
of a great contentment, the restful peace of God.'[11]

No wonder Paul says, 'Godliness with contentment is
great gain' (1 Tim 6:6). An attractive quality and one
which encourages growth. He links *godliness* with contentment. That is important. Leave God out and con-

tentment can become complacency, which has in it a sense of self-sufficiency and smugness which is far removed from God-centred Christian contentment.

The sin of discontent

Before looking at two passages in the New Testament which give us the secret of contentment, I want to think about the sin of discontent. To see something of the destructive nature of this, as well as seeing the attractive nature of contentment, may be a great incentive to seeking the secret of contentment.

You may be asking, 'Isn't there a holy discontent?' Perhaps there is, but I am talking about *unholy* discontent! We can recognize it by its spirit and by what it leads to. There is in it a spirit of frustration, self-pity, impatience and complaining. There is usually a tendency to blame either God or man, and it leads, as we shall see, to a rebellious spirit against God, or to envy and coveting. If there is such a thing as holy discontent, it will not contain any of that spirit, and it will lead to submission to God and to positive action. Paul was not contented with how far he had gone in the Christian race, but there was none of the spirit I have described and it led him to positive and active pressing on (see Philippians 3:12-14).

Discontent is certainly not an atmosphere that encourages growth. It is also terribly infectious. There is a solemn word in Jude's letter about this. He is writing about people who cause divisions in the church and in verse 16 (RSV) he writes, 'These are grumblers, malcontents . . . .' In a school staff room, in an office, in a church, in any community of people, one grumbler or malcontent can infect others until discontent becomes widespread and divisive.

It started in the Garden of Eden. It resulted from

Satan's pernicious lie whispered into Eve's ear. 'God knows that when you eat of it your eyes will be opened, and you will be like God, knowing good and evil' (Gen 3:5). In other words, 'God is not good, he is depriving you of that which he knows would be good for you.' And so there followed the discontent with what God had given and the coveting of that which he had forbidden, leading to the taking of the fruit, the giving to her husband and then the long, long trail of disaster which has followed.

We see it again outstandingly in the story of the people of Israel in the wilderness. After four hundred years of slavery in Egypt, God had wonderfully delivered them and promised to bring them into a rich homeland, the land of Canaan. In spite of this, they were barely across the Red Sea, miraculously set free, before they became discontented and started their grumbling and complaining against Moses. And so they went on finding things to grumble about all through those forty years in the wilderness. Incidentally, if they had not grumbled they would have got into the Promised Land much more quickly. It was when they were on the edge of going in and the spies came back to report on what they had seen, that they were discontented with the description of the land to which they were going and began to grumble against Moses. Later, the Lord said about them, 'How long will this wicked community grumble against me? I have heard the complaints of these grumbling Israelites' (Num 14:27). This resulted in the Lord turning them back into the wilderness for what was almost another forty years. Writing to the Corinthians, Paul uses that part of the people of Israel's history as a warning against four sins which they committed: idolatry, immorality, putting God to the test and grumbling. Would you or I put a discontented grumbling spirit in the same category as idolatry and immorality?

We know only too well that these stories are by no means out of date. Have you ever caught yourself listening to Satan's lie, 'God is depriving you of that which he knows would be good for you'? Someone says, 'Why did God not give me better opportunities as a young person when he knew it would have meant that I could have served him better?' Another says, 'Why didn't God allow me to get married when he knew I was the kind of person who needed it?' Or it may take the form of those two little words, 'If only . . . .'

    If only I had someone else's position
    If only I had someone else's gifts
    If only I had someone else's opportunities
    If only I had someone else's education
    If only I had someone else's health
    If only I had someone else's possessions
    If only I were married
    If only I were single!
    If only . . . .

Some years ago, round Christmas-time, there was a picture in *Punch* which caricatured this whole matter of discontent. It pictured a large store and out of the toy department were coming a number of children with their mothers. Each mother was carrying in one hand a toy for her child and with the other hand was holding one of the child's hands. Every one of the children was doing the same thing: crying and bellowing, and with its free hand pointing at one of the other children's toys! We have all seen that tendency in children, but do we not have to admit that though we conceal it better than children do we are still capable of that kind of spirit?

Even when we think about those Israelites in the wilderness and feel how wrong they were to grumble so much and to give way to discontent so often, are we ourselves much better than they? Christians have experienced a far greater deliverance than theirs. Through the Lord Jesus we have been delivered from the slavery of guilt and from Satan's power. In the cross we have been given a far greater demonstration of God's love, and he has given us far greater promises. Should these facts not be a tremendous incentive to us *not* to be like them, but to seek the secret of that deep contentment which is so encouraging to growth and so beautiful a characteristic?

The secret of contentment

Opening our hearts to receive God's forgiveness for all our past discontent and grumbling, let us now look at two passages in the New Testament which speak about contentment. One is about being content with what we have; the other about being content whatever our circumstances.

Contentment with possessions

The writer of the letter to the Hebrews says,

> Keep your lives free from the love of money and be content with what you have, because God has said, 'Never will I leave you; never will I forsake you.' So we say with confidence, 'The Lord is my helper; I will not be afraid. What can man do to me?' (Heb 13:5-6)

Discontent with money and the things money can buy has been prevalent all down the ages (John the Baptist told soldiers to be content with their pay in Luke 3:14!), and it is certainly a mark of our society today. Again, Christians cannot claim that the same spirit does not creep into our hearts at times. Does this mean that we should never desire anything? No, there are natural desires which are not at all wrong in themselves. It is when these desires lead to a rebellious spirit towards God or envy of others or even dislike of others who have what we do not have, that the sin of discontent is creeping in.

The reason the writer to the Hebrews gives for keeping ourselves free from the love of money and for being content with what we have, is that God has said, 'Never will I leave you; never will I forsake you.' To go back into the Old Testament context of that promise helps to give force to what is being said. We need to go back to the time when Moses was handing over his leadership of the Israelites to Joshua. He was giving Joshua strong words of encouragement, reminding him that the Lord would be with him and ending with these words, 'He will never leave you nor forsake you' (Deut 31:8). Later, when Moses had died and Joshua was entering into the great responsibility of leadership, the Lord himself repeated these words to him and added a statement which to me fills the promise with good things. The Lord said, 'As I was with Moses, so I will be with you; I will never leave you or forsake you' (Josh 1:5). In effect God was saying, 'I will be the same person to you as I was to Moses; I will be to you what I was to him. In the same way as I did not fail or forsake him I will not fail or forsake you.'

What is the name of the One who is speaking? Moses asked this question when God called him and the answer he received was, 'This is what you are to say to the Israelites: "I AM has sent me to you" . . . this is my name' (Exod 3:14-15). I AM—the eternal, unchanging One; the One who becomes to his people all that they need. He is the very same One to us, and his name is *Jesus*; the One who, when here on earth said, 'Before Abraham was born, I am' (Jn 8:58). No wonder the writer to the Hebrews said in the same passage as we are looking at: 'Jesus Christ is the same yesterday and today and for ever' (Heb 13:8). So we can confidently know that he says the same to us as he said to them.

What then had he been to Moses? Moses himself tells us in Deuteronomy. These were some of the things he said: 'The Lord watched over us; he led us; he fought for us; he provided for us; he *loved* us; we have lacked nothing.' These are the things the Lord assured Joshua he would never stop doing for him and these are the things the Lord Jesus will never stop doing for us. He will never leave or forsake us as the One who will watch over us, lead us, fight for us, provide for us and, above all, love us.

We have listened to Moses speaking, now let us listen to him singing. He gave a wonderful song to the people before he left them, which is given to us in Deuteronomy 32. It would take much longer to sing this song than it does to sing most of our modern Christian songs, and we cannot go through it all here. There is one name that he gives to God three times in this song. He sings, 'I will proclaim the name of the Lord. Oh, praise the greatness of our God! He is the Rock' (Deut 32:3-4). When we think of that name in relation to the wilderness journey, it must have spoken to them of a place where they could find shelter from the sun, where they could be lifted up above their enemies and a place in which there were often great deep caves where they could take refuge. It speaks above all of safety, of security. God was assuring Joshua that he would never leave nor forsake him as his safety, his security, his place of refuge in the days that lay ahead. Jesus Christ is the same today; the One who will never fail to be our Rock in which we can take refuge from all our enemies, in all our storms, our final security in life and through death.

We have listened to Moses speaking and singing; now let us listen to him praying. If we really want to know what someone's relationship with the Lord is like, we need to be able to listen to that one in prayer alone with the Lord. Of course that is not possible today but in the Bible we have recorded for us the private prayers of some of God's children and of the Lord Jesus himself. Moses is one of these and so we are allowed into that sacred place where he withdrew himself to speak to the Lord. The occasion was the return of the spies after they had been sent to bring back a report on the Promised Land. Ten of them had brought back an evil report and immediately the people were grumbling again, and cried out against Moses and God. God said that he would disinherit them and make of Moses a greater nation. So Moses prayed, and boldly told God that he could not do this! Because of his promise and for the sake of his reputation, he could not cast them off. Then, reminding the Lord that he had revealed himself as one slow to anger, abounding in love and forgiving sin and rebellion, he pleaded with God to forgive them, and ended with these words: 'Forgive the sin of these people, just as you have pardoned them from the time they left Egypt until now' (Num 14:10-19). Moses knew how much there had been to forgive: the grumbling, the rebellion, the denial of God's love 'from the time they left Egypt until now'.

When the Lord spoke to Joshua, he wanted him to know that he who had forgiven in the past would not leave or forsake him—the One who would continue to forgive in his abounding love.

Can money buy any of these things which are assured to us by the Lord Jesus when he says to *us*, 'Never will I leave you, never will I forsake you'?

Can money buy his love? Can money buy his guidance, his provision and protection? Can money buy the security his presence brings? Can money buy his forgiveness? Never.

A glorious fact is that the more we value and have our

eyes on these wonderful things which money cannot buy, the more contented we shall be with what we have.

After that quotation, 'Never will I leave you; never will I forsake you', the writer to the Hebrews says, 'So we say with confidence, "The Lord is my helper; I will not be afraid. What can man do to me?"' He was remembering that in their early days the Christians to whom he was writing had faced suffering for Christ's sake, and in Hebrews 10:34 he says, 'You joyfully accepted the confiscation of your property, because you knew that you yourselves had better and lasting possessions.' But now some of them were in danger of drifting and turning back from their allegiance to Christ, possibly fearing further suffering and loss for his sake. He wants to remind them that with the utterly reliable word of the Lord Jesus, he will never leave nor forsake them, they have these better and lasting possessions which no man can take from them, and can say with confidence whatever the future might hold, 'The Lord is my helper; I will not be afraid.'

In these days of economic recession, inflation, redundancy and unemployment, there may be very real fear and anxiety connected with your particular type of discontent over money and material things. If so, can you feast your heart afresh on his promise that he will never leave nor forsake you, and on those better and lasting possessions which cannot be taken from you? Whatever comes, he who is the same yesterday, today and for ever will guide you, provide for you, and protect you. He will be your final security and refuge; and above all—nothing, nothing will rob you of his forgiving love.

Contentment whatever our circumstances

In Philippians 4:11-13 Paul says, 'I have learned to be content whatever the circumstances. . . . I have learned the secret of being content in any and every situation. . . . I can do everything through him who gives me strength.' The Good News Bible translates that last phrase as, 'I have the strength to face all conditions by the power that Christ gives me.' J. B. Phillips paraphrases it as, 'I am ready for anything through the strength of the One who lives within me.'

In writing about this Ralph Martin says:

> This statement, then, does not make Paul a wonder-worker, a spiritual 'super-man', who towers so far above the rest of men that his life is no encouragement to lesser mortals . . . here was a man who had boundless confidence in the ability of Christ to match every situation.'[12]

Paul is not really claiming that there is nothing he cannot *do*, but he is claiming that there is no situation he cannot *face* and be content in, through the inner strength Christ gives him.

It is still a tremendous claim Paul makes! 'I have learned to be content whatever the circumstances . . . I have learned the secret of being content in any and every situation.' We need to be clear, too, that this contentment is not a passive resignation, which is inconsistent with fighting evil or with taking appropriate action to change a situation. But it does mean an attitude which leads to *God-directed* action, and action timed by God, rather than action directed and timed by our own frustration and discontent.

I am so grateful that twice he said, 'I have learned.' This contentment was not part of his natural temperament, he had to learn it, and so do we. These lessons are not easy to learn. Only by the strength he gives us can they be learned.

What was the school in which he learned this contentment? It was the school of life with all its changes and all

56

its ups and downs. For Paul it was sometimes plenty, sometimes want; sometimes sickness, sometimes health; sometimes popularity, sometimes hostility; sometimes in prison, sometimes free. It is the changes in life that are the most difficult to adapt to, but it is in these that we learn the secret of facing any situation with the contentment that the Lord's inner strength makes possible. Roger Hurding, suffering from recurrent attacks of blindness due to diabetes, bears testimony to the difficulty of the changes: 'He said to God, "I really am prepared to accept either sight or blindness, but please let's settle for one or the other"'![13] What a miracle of the Lord's in-strengthening that this doctor has been able to accept both, and be kept from the bitterness which would inevitably have hindered growth into wholeness.

I wonder what classroom you are in just now? Difficult circumstances? Painful circumstances? All kinds of unexpected interruptions to the peaceful flow of life? All kinds of changes? Or possibly it is the opposite of changes. It may be an extremely difficult situation which goes on and on without any change, till you groan, 'If only. . . .' 'If only my circumstances would change, I'd be contented.' Can you grasp the fact that it is *in* these circumstances, not out of them, that you will learn? A horse is not given jumping lessons in a sheltered stable. It is taken out to face the hurdles!

What lessons did Paul learn which made it possible for him to be contented in any situation and which we need to learn if we, too, are to know that contentment?

There must be many lessons which contributed towards Paul's ability to be content. We shall think about three which are possibly the most basic of all.

The first is best illustrated in the life of Paul's Teacher, the Lord Jesus Christ himself, the second and third come from Paul's own writings.

God is Sovereign Lord over all our circumstances

Jesus said, 'Everyone who is fully trained will be like his teacher' (Lk 6:40). Paul had been a long time in the training school of his Teacher by the time he wrote to the Philippians, and was undoubtedly becoming increasingly like him. Through all his difficult and often painful and dangerous experiences, we see one who was convinced that God was in control of all his circumstances. Therefore he was able to press through all second causes and accept every situation as it came and to submit to God in each situation, knowing that it was the perfect will of God for him at that moment.

This is wonderfully illustrated during the whole earthly life of the Lord Jesus and in all his changing circumstances. Just before he gave the invitation, 'Come to me all you who are weary and burdened,' he had turned to his Father and said, 'I praise you, Father, Lord of heaven and earth' (Mt 11:25,28). He knew that his Father was also Lord, the final authority, in control of every situation which came into his life, the One whose will it was his delight to submit to, and to do. With this in mind, let us watch him and listen to him as he walked the last part of the path that led to the cross.

Think of him first in the Garden of Gethsemane, suffering terrible anguish as he looked ahead. Three times over, with increasing earnestness, he cried to his Father, 'Father, if you are willing, take this cup from me; yet not my will but yours be done' (Lk 22:42). At last the conflict was over and John tells us that when Peter started to use his sword to prevent Jesus from being taken, Jesus commanded Peter to put away his sword and then added, 'Shall I not drink the cup the Father has given me?' (Jn 18:11).

W. E. Sangster referring to these words of Jesus says:

One can transform the contents of a cup if one can change the hand from which one takes it. It is as though the Lord said: 'If I must drink it, I will not take it from Judas, Pilate, Caiaphas or the people—I will take it only from my Father . . . .'[14]

It was in the strength of this that, submitting to *his Father's will*, he allowed them to lead him away. We move on to see him standing before Pilate. Pilate, fearing the people, uneasy in his conscience and exasperated by the silence of Jesus, asked him the question, 'Don't you realise I have power either to free you or to crucify you?' To which Jesus, with quiet authority answered, 'You would have no power over me if it were not given to you from above' (Jn 19:10-11). No doubt Pilate knew that his authority to pass the death sentence came from Rome, from Caesar; it was delegated authority. But Jesus was looking at a higher authority than that of Caesar: the authority of God, from whom all authority is given. The disciples, after Pentecost, did not hesitate to refer to that highest authority when they gathered for prayer and described this very scene. They said:

> Sovereign Lord . . . Herod and Pontius Pilate met together with the Gentiles and the people of Israel in this city to conspire against your holy servant Jesus, whom you anointed. They did *what your power and will had decided beforehand should happen* (Acts 4:27-28 italics mine).

I remember once driving from the east to the west of England to speak at a meeting. I had every intention of bringing into my message this incident in the life of Jesus. As I travelled, I came to a narrow part of the road and in front of me was a van. Mile after mile it went at a slower speed than I wanted to go. When it slowed down going up hills and I could easily have passed, the road always seemed too winding, and when it went down hill, it rattled away at such a speed that, again, passing did not feel safe. Gradually, frustration rose inside me and anxiety as to whether I would arrive on time. I was by no means contented in those circumstances and grumbled away to myself.

Suddenly, I found a question coming into my mind: 'Aren't you going to say at the meeting that nothing could have power over us except it is given from above? What about this van?' This may seem a trivial incident, but it taught me a lesson. I realized that unless I was able to trust God's control over all my circumstances and learn contentment amid the small irritations of life, I would never learn to find it in the more difficult and painful situations.

This is not an easy lesson to learn. Our sinless Saviour went through the agony of Gethsemane before he came out into the deep acceptance which was expressed in those words, 'Shall I not drink the cup the Father has given me?' He understands the struggles we who are by no means sinless often go through before we can reach that place of deep peace and contentment. Our human reactions to our difficult circumstances are often at first those of anger, frustration, resentment or fear. We have to work through these reactions before we can, at an emotional level, accept our situation from the hand of the Father. The vital thing is that we should be open and honest with him about our feelings, so that he who so loves and understands us will handle them for us.

The psalmist said, 'I pour out my complaint before him' (Ps 142:2). There are many instances in the Bible of God's people doing this. It is when we follow their example that he changes our experience of the circumstances and brings his peace.

God is at work in all our circumstances

In Romans 8:28 Paul says, 'We know that in all things God works for the good of those who love him, who have been called according to his purpose.' It is sad that this verse has been quoted so frequently that to many Christians it has lost its force. 'Don't forget Romans 8:28,' we say lightly to someone who is going through some agonizing situation. 'I suppose I must remember Romans 8:28,' we say resignedly when we ourselves are finding our circumstances uncomfortable or painful.

Can we try to recapture something of the triumphant certainty with which Paul wrote these words? If we read the context, we find that Paul is not talking about easy situations but about groaning (v.23) and later on he is talking of trouble and hardship, persecution, famine, danger, the sword (v.35). And finally he ends the chapter with his mighty conviction that nothing 'will be able to separate us from the love of God that is in Christ Jesus our Lord.' Paul knew so deeply that nothing can separate us from God's love that he equally as deeply knew that God in his love is at work in all our circumstances for our good, our highest good.

When Paul said 'all things' he meant '*all* things'. He did not mean all things except the thing that is making you groan today! He did not mean all things except the particular trouble or hardship which you or I may be experiencing today! The Spirit who inspired him could look down all the centuries and, knowing the total sum of what that 'all' would contain, breathed into Paul's heart saying, 'Paul, do not say "in some things" say "in all things",' and he knew what your particular 'all things' would include today!

Paul is quite clear as to what the most important part of 'our good' is. In the next verse (Rom 8:29), he speaks of God's purpose for us, which is that we should be 'conformed to the likeness of his Son'; that we should be made more like Jesus—and that as we have seen is *wholeness*. God is, as Jeremiah saw him, like a potter who takes the marred clay into his skilful and tender hands and uses the wheel of circumstances to mould it into the shape he wants. The model in front of him is the Lord Jesus Christ himself in all his beauty (see Jeremiah 18:1-5).

Could there be any higher good than that? Could there be anything more likely to bring contentment with our circumstances than to lay hold by faith (we will not *see* it happening) of the fact that God has committed himself to work in all things for our good; above all, to be making us more like our Lord Jesus.

God can be thanked in all our circumstances

This third lesson is a very practical one. It comes from Paul's first letter to the Thessalonians. He writes, among other practical instructions: 'Give thanks in all circumstances' (5:18). Find something to thank God for in all circumstances. There is always something for which we can thank him. To thank him that he is sovereign Lord over our circumstances; to thank him that he understands our struggles; to thank him that nothing can separate us from his love and that in his love he is at work in our circumstances for our good, is the greatest contribution we can make towards those great facts getting a deeper grip of us. And if we look for them, there are always other things to thank him for.

Years ago, I was greatly helped by a letter printed in a Christian magazine. The man who wrote the letter was talking about thanking God and said something to the effect that while we cannot always *feel* like rejoicing or praising, we can always say 'thank you'. That may not sound very grand when Paul, writing to the Philippians said, 'Rejoice in the Lord always,' but it can be the first rung on the ladder towards turning a negative experience into a more positive one, and it may end in being able to rejoice in the Lord. Paul did not say, 'Rejoice in your feelings,' or 'in your circumstances', but 'in the Lord' (Phil 4:4).

We have looked at the classroom; we have looked at some of the lessons; now let us turn our eyes afresh on Paul's Teacher and ours, the Lord Jesus Christ. Remember that Paul said it was 'through the strength of the One who lives in me' that he had learned these lessons and could face any situation with contentment. The teaching of the Lord Jesus is different from that of any other teacher for he writes his lessons on our hearts and, by his power within us, does the work of changing us and changing our experience of the situation. It is as we submit ourselves to him, in all our weakness, with the desire that he should teach us, that we shall begin to learn, in all the situations we face, something of the secret of being content whatever our circumstances.

We have seen that all growth takes place in relationships, and that our relationship with God is the one absolutely vital one. We have also seen that his relationship with us is above all a relationship of love (see 1 John 4:19).

To sum up then: let us think about this matter of contentment in terms of his wonderful love for us. He loves us enough to commit himself never to leave us nor forsake us, with all that that includes of spiritual possessions, as well as provision for our bodily needs.

More amazing still, he loves us enough to come and live in each one of us, writing his truth on our hearts and giving us his own strength to make it possible for us to face every situation with the quality of contentment which would be quite impossible apart from him.

5

MARTHA AND MARY

Two Sisters and Their Growing Relationship with Jesus

Looking at the three stories in which these two sisters appear in the gospels, we have living examples of people who grew through their relationship with the Lord Jesus and with one another.

We see in both their lives a developing relationship with Jesus; a developing relationship with one another and increasing likeness to their Friend and Master.

Before we look at each of the stories in turn, there is one fact that is very important for us to notice. The two sisters were different and remained different. In each story Martha was on her feet and Mary was at the feet of Jesus. Martha seems to have been the more active, Mary the more contemplative. And they remained like that. That does not mean that Martha never thought and that Mary was never active, but it does show that they had different temperaments and that Jesus respected this. He does not want us all to be the same. He does not want us all to be like one another. What he does want is to take from us the things that spoil and hinder us from becoming the unique individuals that God intends us to be. That will undoubtedly include certain temperamental changes as we grow, but it will not mean that we will all become the same.

He will make us less self-centred in the expression of our particular temperaments and more Christ-centred. For example, sensitivity linked with self-centredness frequently turns to self-pity; whereas sensitivity linked with Christ-centredness turns much more frequently towards the ability to sympathize with others. The marvel is that while remaining different he does make us all more like himself in character; that is, in such characteristics as love, truth, kindness, humility and contentment. The rainbow is not only made up of every colour, but of every shade of every colour. Roses are all alike in certain distinctive ways, but those likenesses are expressed in a glorious variety of ways. In our church fellowships we need different shades of likeness to Christ if we are to represent his character more and more truly. For instance, love for him and for one another will be expressed in different ways by those of different temperaments, and we should rejoice in these differences.

Now, let us turn to the three stories which are in Luke 10, John 11 and John 12. Each scene took place in Bethany, a village not far from Jerusalem, which was the home of Martha and Mary and their brother Lazarus.

Jesus the teacher

As Jesus and his disciples were on their way, he came to a village where a woman named Martha opened her home to him. She had a sister called Mary, who sat at the Lord's feet listening to what he said. But Martha was distracted by all the preparations that had to be made. She came to him and asked, 'Lord, don't you care that my sister has left me to do the work by myself? Tell her to help me!'

'Martha, Martha,' the Lord answered, 'you are worried and upset about many things, but only one thing is needed. Mary has chosen what is better, and it will not be taken away from her' (Lk 10:38-42).

In this story Jesus taught them both: Martha while she was on her feet, Mary while she sat at his feet. We do not know whether this was Jesus' first visit to the home in Bethany. We do not know whether his visit took the sisters by surprise or not. I think it must have been a surprise visit because if not Martha would probably have made the preparations beforehand. What we do know is that it was Martha who opened her home to him, welcoming him in. We know that the disciples were with him (I doubt whether she left them outside!)—in which case there were thirteen men crowding into her house! Her first thought was that they must be fed, and that this wonderful guest deserved the very best of preparations, so off she rushed to the kitchen. She never stopped to ask him what he most wanted, or whether food was the chief reason for his coming. Her one thought was to express her love in service for him, and he never blamed her for that. So, what went wrong?

First, she became distracted with all the preparations she had to make. The Good News Bible says: 'Upset over all the work she had to do.' She thought of one thing after another. Why had she run out of this? Why hadn't she bought that? Had she got enough of this? Where was that sister of hers? Why wasn't she helping? Being upset led to frustration, annoyance and self-pity, until it exploded into accusation against Jesus, the one she loved! She was angry with him—he should have done something about it! 'Don't you care?' she cried. 'Look at all the work I'm doing for you! And my sister has left me to do it by myself. Tell her to come and help me.'

Can you identify with Martha? I can! Pressure of work —so much to do, so little time to do it in, nobody to help and the one whom we feel should be helping involved in something else, possibly something that we feel makes her (or him) look more spiritual. So we get more and more upset, self-pity floods in, till rising frustration and anger cause us to hurl the blame at someone or something. Inside ourselves we are saying, 'Lord, don't you care?' We women can easily identify with Martha in her kitchen, but it is a mistake to think that *only* women can identify with Martha's feelings. In our activity-centred world, in which we tend so easily to feel our worth depends on what we *do* rather than on what we *are*, the spirit of Martha can easily take hold of men or women— at home, in secular work, or in what we call our Christian service.

Now listen to the Teacher: first, *he gave Martha a tender rebuke*. 'Martha, Martha.' Can you hear the tone of his voice? His rebukes are always tender, always filled with compassion and understanding. Then, *he told her she was doing too much*. 'You are worried and upset about many things, but only one thing is needed.' We do not always like it when people tell us we are doing too much. It seems to suggest that they do not realize the importance of our activities! I suspect that sometimes, perhaps frequently, we shut our eyes to the Lord when he says to us, 'You are doing too much. *I* don't require you to do so much.' Possibly, we are more likely to shut our ears when he speaks through some human channel.

Lastly, *he said that Mary was right*. That must have been a hard pill for Martha to swallow. He said that Mary had chosen what was better and that it would not be taken from her. Remember that it was Jesus who said Mary was right. I have not infrequently met those who sympathize with Martha and are somewhat impatient with Mary. Certainly we can understand Martha and identify with her, but if we are too much in sympathy with her then we are out of sympathy with Jesus and failing to understand that which he most desired. Praise

God for all those who are active, practical and busy like Martha; and praise God that many of those find the way, as we shall see Martha did, to be able to serve without the spirit she showed in this story. Through it all, do not forget the tenderness of Jesus' rebuke. I am sure that it was because of the tenderness of his teaching that she was able to change.

Let us now look at Mary as she sat at the Lord's feet listening to him. *She knew what he most wanted.* It is important, is it not, to find out what our guests want, not what we think they want. When we were in Kenya, some of our friends teased me in an affectionate way, telling me that whenever guests arrived at our home, the first thing I asked was whether they wanted a bath! When I came in hot and dusty off the road that was what I most wanted, but it was not always what the guest most wanted!

It is possible to concentrate so much on the fact that Mary was doing what *she* wanted to do, that we forget that it was what *Jesus* most wanted. How do we know that? We hear God say through the psalmist, 'My people . . . how I wish you would listen to me' (Ps 81:8 GNB). We turn to the prophets and, all the way through, sense something of the heartbreak of God because his people would not listen to him. Jesus knew that all his words, all his teaching came from God; to listen to him was to listen to God. He knew the pain of hostility towards his teaching, indifference towards his teaching, people taking offence at his teaching. Only occasionally in the gospels do we find people like the woman of Samaria, Nicodemus and Mary drinking in his teaching and, for the moment, dropping everything else that they were doing. What joy it must have given him! This is what he hungered for more than food.

She also knew that Jesus had lessons to teach which she needed to learn and that no one else could teach her. Who

69

else could teach her about God? What God is like, what God requires of man? Who else could teach her the real meaning of life? Who else could teach her what Jesus himself had come to do? His teaching was so different from that of all her religious teachers, it had an inner authority which theirs lacked.

These are some of the great things we need to learn from him. There is also a constant need to listen to him and learn from him in the practical details of life. In relationship problems, in work situations, in bringing up a family, in difficult decisions that need to be made, how we need to hear what he is saying. When I want to hear what he is saying about some situation and do give time to bring it to him, my experience is not one of hearing a voice, or finding some verse from the Bible jump out at me (though others may have such experiences). It is usually one of some unexpected thought coming which breaks the vicious circle of my own thinking on the subject, and which shows a way that is different from any I had thought of. I have come to recognize that this is his way of teaching me.

Because she knew what he most wanted and what she most needed, *Mary found time to sit at his feet and to listen to him*. For the time being, she dropped every other activity and gave herself up entirely to listening to his teaching.

I know that the Lord Jesus teaches us, as he did Martha, when we are active about our work, whether that happens to mean being on our feet or in some other position; but there is a tremendous need for us to find time to drop all our usual activities and to concentrate on him. My own experience and that of numbers of other Christians tells me that it is abundantly worth while to find some time daily to drop other activities and to sit at his feet. I am not saying, 'You must,' in the sense that

God will not bless your day if you do not find that time. I am saying that it is one of the richest contributions towards our growth. And if the Lord longs that we should give him time, then he can help us to look at our whole programme and give us ideas as to how we can find the time.

It may be that finding time is not a problem to you, but that there is not sufficient desire. If so, can you get hold of the fact that the Lord Jesus longs that you should give him time? Start to do it to please him, and I think it will not be long before you discover the benefits and begin to form a most valuable habit. In any close relationship it is lovely to do things together; to work together, to play together, but if the relationship is to grow and flourish, it is necessary to find time just to sit down and share together.

In these times with him, his chief way of speaking to us and teaching us is through the Bible. There is no substitute for this, and we are privileged to have many simple aids to regular Bible reading and to gaining an understanding of the Bible. We are also privileged to have translations of the Bible which use modern English, and which have made the Bible live to many who found the older language difficult to understand.

Remember that Jesus said, 'I praise you, Father, Lord of heaven and earth, because you have hidden these things from the wise and learned, and revealed them to little children' (Mt 11:25). We do not need to be clever or intellectual in our Bible reading. What we do need is a simple child-like attitude of mind that is eager to learn. Little children are eager to learn; it is older ones who are sometimes not so eager! Mary's teacher is our Teacher. Though we cannot see him, he by his Spirit is the One who opens up the Bible and teaches us through it. There are those who say, 'I've been reading the Bible, but I don't seem to get anything out of it.' There is a feeling that unless some exciting truth springs out of the part read, or some particular words 'speak' to them the reading has had no effect. I have a great longing to say, 'Read it, read it, asking the Holy Spirit who is the Spirit of Jesus to teach you, and the effects of that teaching will be far greater than you realize at the time.'

Working among drug addicts in the walled city of Hong Kong, Jackie Pullinger saw the effects of teaching the Bible to the many who were wonderfully brought to know the Lord. Many were unable to read and had no homes other than the streets, but she found that a vital part of their growth was for her to begin to read the Bible with them. For most of us, conditions are very easy by comparison. We should look upon our comparative ease as a privilege and make the most of it.

Mary, sitting at the feet of Jesus to listen to his teaching, also speaks of submission and intention to obey. A friend of Mark Twain's is reported to have said to him that he was troubled by the parts of the Bible that he could not understand, to which Mark Twain replied that it was the parts that he could understand which troubled him! The parts he could understand challenged him to obey. What a comfort it is to realize that the teaching of the Lord Jesus is an inner teaching, or writing on our hearts by his Spirit, which gives the power to obey. We have that wonderful promise in Ezekiel 36:26-27 where God says (speaking of the time when his Spirit would come and live within every believer), 'I will give you a new heart and a new mind. I will take away your stubborn heart of stone and give you an obedient heart. I will put my spirit in you and I will see to it that you follow my laws and keep all the commands I have given you' (GNB). His teaching includes doing this work in us. There may be times when we feel that not only have we not got the strength to obey, but we are not even sure that we wholly want to; part of us does, part of us does not. At those times, we can bring ourselves to him as we are, in all our weakness, asking that he will work in us both to will and to act according to his will (Phil 2:13).

Jesus the comforter

In John 11 we have the story of the message sent to Jesus about the sickness of Lazarus, brother of Martha and Mary; and Jesus' delay in going to them which resulted in the death of Lazarus. We read of Jesus' encounter with both Martha and Mary and then the wonderful moment when they received their brother back from the grave. In this setting we see them entering into a new phase in their relationship with the Lord Jesus. I do not think they would have found him as their Comforter in these circumstances had they not learned to relate to him as Teacher when life was peaceful and happy.

Let us first look at their suffering, for they were both suffering. They were suffering the loss of a much-loved brother and, at the same time, they were disappointed and perplexed. They had sent a message to Jesus to say that Lazarus was ill. They knew he could heal those who were sick. Surely he would come immediately and heal their brother. Yet he delayed; a delay long enough for all hope to fade away and for them to watch their brother die. They were suffering bereavement—the end of a precious human relationship—and they were suffering perplexity in their relationship with Jesus. 'Why, why had he not come in time?' If only he had come in time, he could have done something. And they had let him know in time. A doctor may rightly say that even if he had come in time, there was nothing he could have done; but not this Physician. One touch, one word, and their brother would have been healed. What would we have felt like?

There are experiences other than that of the death of one we love which are similar to bereavement. Some form of loss is at the bottom of much human suffering. 'I feel as if I'd been bereaved,' said a lady who had changed her job after fifteen years in a very happy situation. If that suffering is mixed with perplexity it is much more difficult to bear, especially if the perplexity and perhaps disappointment is caused by failure to understand what God is doing because of delay on his part.

The first lesson we can learn from this story is that times like these, times of suffering and perplexity, are opportunities to grow in our relationship with Jesus; opportunities to find him in a new way, to experience him as the One who shows us what the God of all comfort is like. Let us look then at Martha and Mary and see what happened.

First and most important: they both went to Jesus. Each went in her own way—Martha upright on her feet, Mary to his feet and in tears. When they reached him, they did not start by talking about the sorrow of their bereavement, they both started by telling him their feelings about his delay. 'Lord, if you had been here my brother would not have died.'

That they both went to Jesus about their sorrow sounds simple and obvious, does it not? Who would they go to but him? But is it always easy? Do we always find it easy to go to him and pour out all we feel? All the hurt, all the perplexity, perhaps the anger; particularly when we feel that the deepest hurt is to do with *him*. Can we learn that to do this is what he wants and that it is the pathway to healing and comfort? As the story goes on, we see how he brought comfort to each of the sisters, first separately and then together.

Martha was the first to go out to meet him. She not

only expressed her pain and perplexity, she added a note of trust and desperate hope. 'I know that even now God will give you whatever you ask.' Even now! When humanly speaking all hope had gone and Lazarus was dead, Martha had a spark of hope. She obviously had not nursed any resentment against Jesus because of his previous rebuke. Neither had she lost her trust in his attitude towards her. She was not saying, as we might, 'He didn't think much of my behaviour on that occasion when he came to our home, I doubt whether he will want to have much to do with me just yet.' There was trust and a spark of hope.

In response to Martha's coming to him, he gave her a wonderful assurance: 'Your brother will rise again.' Then, when Martha thought that he meant on the last day but not now, he gave her a wonderful revelation: 'I am the resurrection and the life. He who believes in me will live, even though he dies; and whoever lives and believes in me will never die' (Jn 11:25-26). He was saying something like this: 'Martha, even now Lazarus is alive and I am here. We do not need to wait till the last day to summon him back; but whether or not I summon him back now makes no difference to the fact that he is living. And, Martha, from now on countless believers are going to remember what I have said to you, and are going to rejoice that those who believe in me, and who others say have died, are living; yes, living!'

He then asked her whether she believed this. Her immediate response was, 'Yes, Lord. . . .' Notice that she did not say, 'Yes, Lord, I believe what you have said.' She said, 'Yes, Lord, I believe that you are the Christ, the Son of God, who was to come into the world.' She believed in *him*, the Person behind the words, so of course she believed what he said. Her confession of conviction about him was as full a one as anyone gave during his earthly life.

There was no sign in Martha of resentment towards Jesus and there was also none towards her sister, Mary. After talking with Jesus, she went back and quietly said to Mary, 'The Teacher is here . . . and is asking for you.' The Teacher—what title could have appealed to Mary more than that one? In response to that message, Mary got up quickly and went to Jesus. Falling at his feet in tears, she said the same words as Martha had said, 'Lord, if you had been here, my brother would not have died.' Did he explain his delay? Did he solve her perplexity? No; but she saw that 'He was deeply moved in spirit and troubled' (Jn 11:33). That expression includes both indignation and sympathy visible in Jesus.

William Hendriksen says:

> The intense upsurge of emotion was probably visible in Christ's look, tone of voice, and (perhaps *especially*) in his constant sighing. . . . Indignant with sin as the root of all suffering and sorrow, but also taking to heart the sorrow of those about him, . . . Jesus, thus deeply moved in the spirit . . . and visibly agitated, said, 'Where have you laid him?'[15]

And then she saw his tears. There could be no question about his involvement in their suffering. The depth of his feeling was visible in his body and in his tears.

A Christian friend of ours years ago ran a small school for African boys on a farm in East Africa. One of those boys was tragically drowned in a river on the farm. Our friend had to go and break the news to the parents, who were not Christians, and she attended the boy's funeral. Some time later, someone asked the parents what had caused their hearts to open to the Christian message brought by this friend of ours. Their simple reply was, 'She cried when our boy was drowned.' What a comforting and softening power tears can have!

Martha's comfort came through what he said and Mary's came through his involvement in their suffering which was so plainly visible in his expression. And then he acted. The glorious moment came when at the tomb he called to Lazarus to come out, and he came out!

If we can lay hold of certain lessons from this story, we too will grow, even in and through our times of sorrow and perplexity.

1. *When in suffering and perplexity our hearts cry out 'Why?' there is one thing about which we can be sure*

That thing is stated in John 11:5—'Jesus loved Martha and her sister and Lazarus. Yet. . . .' John makes that clear right at the beginning of the story. We are to know that the delay did not mean that he did not love them. Even though he loved them, *still* he delayed. It is a tremendous strength and comfort to know that however perplexing our sorrow may be, or God's seeming delay in coming to us, it does not mean that he does not love us. It is an even greater step of faith to be able to say, 'In some mysterious way which I don't at present understand, this is happening because he *does* love me.'

Notice that he did not rebuke them for questioning his delay.

2. *When he delays it is always because he has some greater revelation of himself to give us and some greater manifestation of his power*

They thought that he would come to heal a sick man because he had revealed himself as the great Healer, the great Physician. *He* intended to reveal himself as the Resurrection and the Life and to raise a dead man to life. It is often through being brought, as the two sisters were, to a place of human hopelessness and helplessness, that we are being prepared for some fresh revelation of himself and of his power. This may help us to accept, even to welcome, the knowledge of our human hopelessness and helplessness in the face of some of the causes of our sorrow and perplexity.

3. *When we take our suffering and perplexity to him we shall know that he is deeply moved*

Jesus is the same yesterday, today and for ever (Heb 13:8). There is still the Man, Christ Jesus, on the throne of heaven who enters into our feelings. He feels with us, he weeps with us.

The results of their relationship with Jesus

Six days before the Passover, Jesus arrived at Bethany, where Lazarus lived, whom Jesus had raised from the dead. Here a dinner was given in Jesus' honour. Martha served, while Lazarus was among those reclining at the table with him. Then Mary took about a pint of pure nard, an expensive perfume; she poured it on Jesus' feet and wiped his feet with her hair. And the house was filled with the fragrance of the perfume. But one of his disciples, Judas Iscariot, who was later to betray him, objected, 'Why wasn't this perfume sold and the money given to the poor? It was worth a year's wages.' He did not say this because he cared about the poor but because he was a thief; as keeper of the money bag, he used to help himself to what was put into it.

'Leave her alone,' Jesus replied. 'It was meant that she should save this perfume for the day of my burial. You will always have the poor among you, but you will not always have me' (Jn 12:1-8).

This is again a happy scene. Lazarus was alive and the family reunited. In honour of Jesus they gave a dinner and the disciples were there. I do not know how many others were invited, but there was certainly a big crowd present, because Jews from Jerusalem came, not just to see Jesus, but to see the remarkable sight of a man who had died and was now alive. I expect our big-hearted and practical Martha felt they must be given some food as well as a look at her brother!

There are only two words about Martha in this story: 'Martha served.' There she was still on her feet, still serving; but no frustration, no sign of being upset (even though there were more guests), no disapproval of Mary for what she did. Surely, thankfulness had got rid of all that. She had grown; Jesus had saved her from those destructive factors which would have hindered her growth and he had also assured her that he is the Saviour from death, that final enemy.

So we leave Martha and find Mary, for the third time, at the feet of Jesus—with a costly gift of love. A beautiful alabaster jar containing very rare, expensive perfume; the jar broken and all the ointment poured over Jesus' feet. Judas said that it was worth a year's wages. Mark tells us that she broke the jar and poured the contents over his head as well as his feet (Mk 14:1-9). Having done this she wiped his feet with her hair, breaking through social custom in the abandonment of her love.

We can best see the stage Mary had reached in her relationship with Jesus, and in her personal growth, by contrasting her with Judas. Judas grumbled about what he regarded as a waste of perfume. According to him it should have been sold and the money given to the poor —a very pious thought! In verse 6 we learn what the real reason for his grumbling was. He was the treasurer of the little group of disciples and he used to help himself to some of the money. 'He used to *take* . . .' the RSV says. Judas is an outstanding example of self-centredness, the basic principle of which is to take. Self-centredness has many subtle ways of hiding and covering itself up. Judas covered up with that pious pretence that he was concerned about the poor! Mary had become Jesus-centred. She had received so much from him that he had become the centre of her life and all she wanted was to give.

It is only in a relationship with Jesus that our basic self-centredness is really changed; that self-centredness which destroys peace has a withering influence and hinders growth. No doubt this out-pouring of love was Mary's way of expressing her gratitude to Jesus for the wonder of the raising of Lazarus. There may also have been an added reason—Matthew's account records that Jesus said, 'She did it to prepare me for burial' (Mt 26:12). Some who comment on this story suggest that Mary knew he was going to die and, instead of keeping the ointment to anoint his dead body, she poured it out beforehand to show him her love and gratitude while he was still alive. If she did realize that he was to die, we do not know how much she understood of the meaning of that death. We certainly have a much richer understanding than she could have had. And it is his love, above all expressed in his death, which is the one power capable of changing us from self-centredness to Christ-centredness, and of causing us to give him the most precious gift we can give, that of ourselves.

Isaac Watts expressed this in his well-known words:

> Were the whole realm of nature mine,
> That were an offering far too small;
> Love so amazing, so divine
> Demands my soul, my life, my all.

'My soul, my life, my all'—more precious than an alabaster jar of costly perfume; more precious than 'the whole realm of nature'.

We have seen these two sisters in a growing relationship

with Jesus. As a result of that growing relationship we can see that they have both become more like the One they loved and to whom they owed so much. Martha is bearing the likeness of him who said, 'I am among you as one who serves' (Lk 22:27). Mary is bearing the likeness of him who 'loved me and gave himself for me' (Gal 2:20).

6

ELIJAH

'A Man Just Like Us'

'I have had enough, Lord' (1 Kings 19:4). It is hard to believe that those words could have come from the mouth of Elijah, that giant of a man, that rugged Old Testament prophet. Yet, it is just at that time in his history that we can most easily see him as 'a man just like us' (Jas 5:17), showing signs of all our human frailty. He was going through a time which is described in Bunyan's *Pilgrim's Progress* as the Slough of Despond. He was downcast, discouraged and almost in despair. He is a great example of the fact that, in the life of God's people, dark times of despondency and discouragement can come, and yet be part of a growing process. We are all liable to these times, we all have our ups and downs; the downs may vary greatly in intensity and length of time, and some people are temperamentally more inclined to go down than others. We read in the Bible of a number of God's people who went through similar times. David, Job and Jeremiah, as well as Elijah, are examples from the Old Testament; and Paul, that great Christian missionary, tells us of a time when he was downcast: 'God who comforts the downcast comforted us' (2 Cor 7:6).

If we read the biographies of outstanding Christian men and women, we find that a number of them also went through their particular dark and despondent times. Never in the Bible did God reproach one who was down. He understands our weaknesses and temperamental tendencies and is always at hand to lift us up and set us on our feet again. In Psalm 37:24 (GNB) the psalmist says, 'If they fall, they will not stay down, because the Lord will help them up.' The important thing is that we should learn and grow as a result of these times. Learning and growth can result in the down times becoming less frequent in our lives and can teach us how to get out of them more quickly when they do come.

Let us look more closely at Elijah, seeking to understand some of the reasons for his state of mind; and then seeing how God treated this discouraged servant of his.

Why was Elijah feeling as he did?

The psalmist asked this question when he was down: 'Why are you downcast, O my soul?' (Ps 42:5). This is a very important question to ask. It is easy to push away our feelings instead of trying with God's help to identify the reason for them. As we think of some of the reasons for Elijah's experience, it may help us to identify likely causes for our own down times. Sometimes, the understanding that comes in answer to the question 'Why?' is the first step to bringing us out, and gives guidelines for practical action, which I shall mention later. At the moment, we are just looking at some of the causes.

First, then, there is no doubt that Elijah was suffering from *reaction after spiritual victory*. The background story is in 1 Kings 17-19. He had experienced miraculous provision. In the midst of famine he had been fed by ravens. He had been used of God to raise a child from the dead. He had seen an amazing and spectacular victory for the Lord over all the false prophets and their god, Baal. He had seen a wonderful answer to prayer for rain after three years of drought. What a record of the Lord's activity in his life! We might think that never again could he possibly be discouraged. Yet he was, and in being so he showed himself to be a man just like us.

We do need to be aware of the frequent tendency to have a reaction after spiritual victory. We have some unusual spiritual blessing, some wonderful answer to prayer, some uplifting meeting or conference, some great victory for the Lord, and then the reaction sets in and down we go. It doesn't always happen, but often it does, and we need to be aware of the possibility and to be on our guard. It is not really surprising that reaction set in, for all the blessing—though wonderful—was costly to Elijah. It was costly physically, it was costly emotionally, and all the time in the background was the intense hostility of the wicked King Ahab and his even more wicked wife, Jezebel. It is possible, in times of great blessing, to forget that we are just frail human beings and that there is bound to be a physical and emotional cost. We also have an enemy, Satan, whose hostility towards us is greater than that of Ahab and Jezebel, and who is eager to get us down and put us out of action.

There was also a *physical element* in his condition. He was overtired. Not only had there been the physical and emotional cost of the victory on Mount Carmel, but he had run about twenty miles in front of Ahab's chariot. Without time to recover his strength, he ran for his life when he heard that Jezebel intended to kill him. Travelling from the north of Israel to the south, he then left his servant and went alone on a day's journey into the desert. It is no wonder that when at last he sat down under a tree, it was not long before he was lying down and fast asleep. That was the best thing that could have happened to him! He did pray before he went to sleep, but it was not a very happy 'goodnight' prayer. He prayed that he might die. It was then that he said to the Lord, 'I have had enough.' I cannot emphasize too strongly the importance of the physical in the conditions that lead to our down times. The state of our bodies affects every other aspect of our personalities, and there is no doubt that overtiredness increases the tendency to be despondent and discouraged.

So, Elijah was suffering from reaction after spiritual victory and great weariness; then the other elements in his condition quickly followed. *He felt totally defeated.* He who had stood so firmly and fearlessly for the Lord on Mount Carmel, alone against all the prophets of Baal, had now received the message of Jezebel's intention to kill him, and had run for his life because of fear. What a terrible defeat and failure he must have felt that to be. Not only had he failed, but he felt himself a total failure —he might as well die.

He was disappointed. It is very disappointing to stand fearless in some situation and then to be overtaken by fear and panic. He showed his disappointment in himself when he said, 'I am no better than my ancestors' (1 Kings 19:4). Had he thought he was! Since he was 'a man like us', and after all the victories he had seen, I can well imagine the thought coming into his mind that there never had been such a prophet in Israel.

Judging by what he later said to the Lord, it seems that he was disappointed in the victory of Mount Carmel. 'The Israelites have rejected your covenant, broken down your altars, and put your prophets to death with the sword. I am the only one left, and now they are trying to kill me too' (1 Kings 19:10). Perhaps he had hoped that the victory would be the beginning of a nationwide revival. Perhaps even Ahab would now know that he must worship the true God and not Baal. As far as he could see, nothing of this had happened. The only visible result was that his own life was in danger, and that would be the end because, in his opinion, he was the only one left who was true to the living God.

Possibly he was disappointed in his God and, with that, some self-pity had crept in. 'I have been very zealous for the Lord God Almighty,' he said. Since he was a man like us, I can again imagine the heart-felt cry, 'Why don't you continue to show yourself on your own behalf and on my behalf as the Lord God Almighty, for whom I have been very zealous?'

He was discouraged. He was discouraged at the state of God's people. He was discouraged at the power of evil in the land. He had no heart left in him and an awful loneliness overcame him. 'I've had enough, Lord, I can't take any more.'

Can we identify with these three feelings of defeat, disappointment and discouragement, as common ingredients in our down times?

Defeat—a consciousness of having failed in some way, perhaps through fear. Then, instead of confessing it to the Lord, receiving his forgiveness, picking ourselves up and going on, we slide downwards: 'I have failed' becomes 'I'm a failure'; this usually leads to a feeling of guilt, then becomes 'I'm worthless'; which leads to 'what's the point—I may as well give up'. This is, in fact, a very common downward spiral.

Disappointment. Disappointment with ourselves. Disappointment that we have failed again. Disappointment that fear, or some other reaction we thought had been conquered, has reared its ugly head again. Disappointment that once again we have proved ourselves to be the frail people we are. Disappointment that we seem to have failed to understand God's will in some situation.

There may be disappointment following what has been

a real spiritual breakthrough, maybe in the life of some friend or relative or in our Christian work or church. A small, struggling church had experienced a time of great spiritual blessing, many members were spiritually renewed, there was fresh life in the services and prayer meetings. They felt they were on the edge of a movement of the Spirit which would reach out to the needy district around. Instead of this, great difficulties arose in a number of individual lives and in the fellowship. Many were deeply disappointed and discouraged.

It is very possible, too, to be disappointed in the Lord, though we find it difficult to admit to that. We may be disappointed that he has not worked in the way we thought he should; disappointed that he has not answered our prayers in the way we had hoped; disappointed that he does not seem to reveal himself and his will to us as he does to others.

Very easily, defeat and disappointment lead to *discouragement*. We lose heart and then the doubts crowd in—doubts about ourselves, doubts about others, doubts about the Lord. This is a lonely experience in which we may echo the words of the psalmist, 'Has his unfailing love vanished for ever? Has his promise failed for all time? Has God forgotten to be merciful? Has he in anger withheld his compassion?' (Ps 77:8-9).

Added to this lonely experience may be the real aloneness of being the only Christian at home, or in our work situation.

Discouragement in our own personal lives can spread to a sense of total discouragement about everything—the state of the world, the state of the church and the rampant powers of evil, as well as negative feelings about those closest to us.

How did God treat Elijah in this experience?

If the key word in Elijah's experience is 'discouragement', the key word in God's handling of his servant is 'encouragement'. Never once did he reproach Elijah. He did not say, 'Elijah, you ought to be ashamed of yourself; after all I've done for you, you ought not to be like this.' He did not say, 'Pull yourself together Elijah, snap out of it.'

The first thing he did was to care for him physically. He gave him the wonderful gift of sleep and then sent an angel to touch him and to feed him. This tender care was repeated twice before he did anything else. Refreshed and strengthened by the sleep and food, Elijah was then taken by God to Horeb, another name for Mount Sinai, the place where God entered into a covenant with his people. There he met with Elijah, the place where he had met with Moses, the place that must have reminded Elijah of all God's purposes of love and of his faithfulness to his people, in spite of their unfaithfulness. There God listened to him. In answer to the question, 'What are you doing here, Elijah?' Elijah poured out his trouble. 'I have been very zealous for the Lord God Almighty. The Israelites have rejected your covenant, broken down your altars and put your prophets to death with the sword. I am the only one left, and now they are trying to kill me too' (1 Kings 19:10).

This was followed by great manifestations of God's power; a mighty wind, an earthquake, a fire; but in none of these did he reveal himself to Elijah. They were followed by 'a gentle whisper'.

The Hebrew is even more picturesque: 'the sound of gentle quietness' or even 'gentle silence'.[16]

God knew that at that moment his servant did not

need those violent manifestations, he needed the gentle quietness. How tenderly he quietened his servant's heart, causing him to pull his cloak over his face in worship. Once again God asked the question, 'What are you doing here, Elijah?' and once again he listened as Elijah poured out his trouble in exactly the same words as before. Perhaps they were spoken more quietly now. Perhaps some of the heat and distress had been taken out by that gentle quietness.

Lastly, God spoke to him, but only after he had cared for him physically, reminded him of his covenant, listened to him and revealed himself to him in gentle quietness.

When God spoke to him, he assured Elijah of the very things for which his heart must have most longed. He assured him that there was still work for him to do; God had not cast him off because of his failure and discouragement. 'Go back,' he said, 'I have got planned service for you; go back and carry on.'

God assured him that he was working out his own purposes in the nation. Elijah had not 'let God down' by his period of despondency and running away, as so many think they have. God had his own plans and purposes, which would be carried out in spite of and even through his servant's ups and downs. In the church of which I wrote earlier, it was evident as time went on that God was working out his own purposes in individuals and in the church as a whole. There was a deepening of spiritual experience and a ministry greater than that of the time when they seemed to be on the crest of a wave.

Finally, he assured him that he was not alone. He was not the only one in the nation who was true to God, there were many who, in hidden ways and places, were true to him. 'I reserve seven thousand in Israel—all whose knees have not bowed down to Baal and all whose mouths have not kissed him' (1 Kings 19:18). Elijah lived to serve God many years after this and when the end of his life on earth came, he who had prayed that he might die never died, for he was taken up to heaven in a whirlwind; a glorious end.

What lessons can we learn from this story which will help us in our own times of despondency and discouragement?

There are three sentences in Psalm 42 which gather these lessons together. In verse 6 the psalmist says, '*My soul is downcast within me.*' He acknowledges his condition.

The first step is to admit to ourselves and to the Lord that we are down. A noticeable fact in the story of Elijah is that he never turned away from the Lord during that dark time, he acknowledged to the Lord the state he was in. As soon as he sat down under the tree, he prayed. And when he said, 'I've had enough, Lord'—he was still relating to him as Lord. We read of King David that his eyes were always towards the Lord; and someone has said that even when he fell, he fell towards the Lord!

One of the most important ways in which our down times can be times of growth is to continue to relate to the Lord in them. We can start by acknowledging our condition to him, even if we are saying, like Elijah, 'I've had enough, Lord.' Often, a sense of guilt keeps us from this. We feel guilty that we feel as we do and ashamed to acknowledge it to the very One who longs to draw near and lift us up.

In verse 5 and verse 11 he asks the question, '*Why are you downcast, O my soul?*'

Having acknowledged our condition, we should ask the question, 'Why?' seeking to identify and face the causes.

Is it reaction after spiritual victory? Are we prepared for this, so that it does not take us by surprise, or take us down into self-condemnation? Can we then deliberately relax and give ourselves time and space to recover physically, emotionally and spiritually? This is often brought about by a short time of complete change of activity.

Is there a physical element? Have we come to recognize that the state of our bodies is closely connected with the down times? Do we take seriously the fact that our bodies are temples of the Holy Spirit (1 Cor 6:19)? The body is an essential part of that which he has bought at such a price. We read that the Lord Jesus said, 'A body you prepared for me' (Heb 10:5). In Psalm 139, we read of how intimately God has been involved in the formation of our bodies. We are responsible for the right care, as well as the right discipline, of our bodies—not least in the matter of rest and food. God's pattern is that there should be a right balance in these things. A balance between work and rest which includes times of recreation, of change of activity, as well as sufficient time for sleep. And, as far as possible, a wisely balanced diet.

There are times when overtiredness cannot be avoided, but very frequently we have to admit that it was doing the unnecessary extra, or perhaps staying up later than was really necessary, which was like 'the last straw'. Some Christians need to learn to be able to say 'No' to certain demands that are made on them!

To take seriously these aspects of our physical needs and to pray about them is an important part of our growth.

The physical aspect is also very important in anyone who suffers from prolonged ill-health or chronic sickness. Times of discouragement are almost inevitable. There is often a tension between two extremes: the one of being too hard on oneself and condemning oneself for being discouraged; the other of being too lenient and excusing all moods on the grounds of ill-health. Only the Lord, who knows and understands us perfectly, can give a right balance and cause the whole experience, including the times of discouragement, to become constructive. David Watson, in both of his autobiographical books (*You Are My God* and *Fear No Evil*), acknowledges the times of discouragement due to chronic ill-health and, finally, terminal sickness. He also says that it was often in those very times of discouragement that the Lord taught some of the most precious lessons.

Has there been defeat leading to a sense of failure? Has that been followed by the downward spiral ending in, 'I may as well give up'? Has the very fact of going down after spiritual victory, or as a result of tiredness, caused a sense of failure? A very important part of our growth is to learn to cope with what we feel are our failures. Sometimes there has been real defeat; sometimes I suspect that God's ideas of what is failure are different from ours. Certainly, he does not want a sense of failure, whatever its reason, to lead to hopelessness. He wants us to learn to receive his forgiveness and his assurance that whatever our failure we are of infinite value to him. He wants us to let him take us by the hand, lift us up and set us on our feet again.

Has disappointment been one of the ingredients of our down times? Disappointment in ourselves? Disappointment in what is happening in God's work? Is there disappointment in God himself?

Has disappointment led to discouragement and all kinds of doubts? We should seek to be honest with ourselves and with God, and do what the psalmist urged us to: 'Pour out your hearts to him' (Ps 62:8).

John the Baptist—the one whom the Lord Jesus called the New Testament Elijah—went through a time of disappointment while in prison; discouragement and doubts about the very one for whom he had prepared the way. He sent a message to Jesus asking, 'Are you the one who was to come, or should we expect someone else?' (Mt 11:3). Writing about this, G. Campbell Morgan says:

> The picture of his dealing with John shows us that honesty is always valued and patiently answered. Let us be true with the Lord; do not let us affect a confidence which our heart does not feel. Only, if the doubt be there, instead of turning our back upon him . . . let us go straight to him and tell him. Oh the comfort of being able to go into the Master's presence and tell him that he is doing something that we cannot understand. He loves honesty. He would rather have the Thomas who blurts out his unbelief, than the Judas who kisses him.[17]

Whatever the answer to the question, 'Why are you downcast?', whether it is one or more of the same factors as were present in Elijah's experience or something different, we must not forget that we have an enemy who is more powerful than Ahab or Jezebel and who is out to take advantage of our down times. In 2 Samuel 7 there is a vivid illustration of our enemy's method. David the king was fleeing from his own son, Absalom, who had taken his throne. Absalom asked for advice from Ahithophel, his chief adviser. He wanted to know the best way to defeat David and bring about his death. This is how Ahithophel started his advice: 'I would attack him when he is weary and weak' (2 Sam 17:2).

That exactly describes Satan's method. He takes advantage of our weariness and weakness to attack us. He is the great accuser. It is good to be able to recognize his voice in the accusations that pester us: 'You're a pretty poor Christian to have got down like this'; 'You're no use in God's service'; 'Are you sure that you really are a Christian?'; 'Are you really sure about anything?' To realize this can be one of the greatest incentives to claim the victory of the Lord Jesus over all Satan's destructive powers; and to affirm our faith in the Lord and our relationship with him, in spite of what we are feeling.

The last of the three sentences in Psalm 42 comes in verse 6: *'Therefore I will remember you.'* The psalmist says, 'My soul is downcast within me; therefore I will remember you.' It seems as if it is not uncommon for us to say, 'My soul is downcast within me; therefore I will forget you'! The discouragement and despondency that we feel is so overwhelming that we lose sight of God. He gets pushed out of the picture. We need to do some deliberate remembering. Remember that he perfectly understands and does not reproach. The accusations do not come from him. Remember that he is concerned about our physical condition and wants us to take the rest and refreshment that we need. Perhaps he wants us to accept help from some human angel! Remember whatever represents the place of the covenant to us; the time or times when he has met with us and we have known that we are his child. Remember all his love and faithfulness to us in spite of all our failure. Above all, let us go to the cross and remember that he gave himself for us. Will he who gave himself for us let us go now?

Then remember that he wants to listen to us. He wants us to be honest about what we feel and he does not mind if we use the same words more than once!

When he has quieted our spirit, he wants to talk to us. He wants to tell us to get up and go back, or perhaps just to go on, for he has loving plans for us which he intends to give us strength to fulfil. What we have learnt and what he has done in us through these dark and difficult times will make greater plans possible, not lesser ones. He wants to assure us that he is well able, by his almighty power, to carry out his own great plans and purposes, and can do this in spite of and even through our times of being down and discouraged.

He wants to assure us that we are not alone. God reminded Elijah that there were several thousand people in Israel who were still true to him. We may *feel* isolated and alone; we may actually *be* isolated and alone, but we are a vital part of an innumerable and world-wide company of God's children, bound together by faith in the Lord Jesus Christ and sharing the life of his Holy Spirit. The remembrance of this can cause us to feel something of the throb of that life and to be encouraged and comforted.

What we learn from God's treatment of Elijah can also give us guidelines in our helping of others in their times of despondency and discouragement. Because of his own Spirit in us, we can be in some measure as understanding, as tender, as quiet, as attentive, as comforting and as encouraging as our God was with his servant.

7

WHAT ABOUT SUFFERING?

God Brings about Growth through Suffering

When I was a very young Christian, as well as young in years, I read a book in which the writer spoke of being so convinced that it is through suffering that we grow and get to know the Lord better, that he described himself as 'ambitious to suffer'. I was eager to grow as a Christian and to get to know the Lord better, so I decided that I must also be 'ambitious to suffer'! I don't think that ambition lasted long but I am grateful that right at the beginning of my Christian life I learned that all spiritual life, and therefore growth, is life out of death. I saw that the cross is woven into the very texture of Christian experience as the Lord takes down into death our self-centredness, in the practical details of our lives. That is a painful process, but the wonderful discovery is that the result is a fresh upspringing of life, his resurrection life.

As the years have passed, I have come to see that just as the suffering of the Lord Jesus which culminated on the cross was transformed into the joy of his resurrection with all its eternal results, so for the Christian all his or her suffering can be transformed, resulting in fresh up-springings of life, leading to growth and increased likeness to the Lord Jesus. This is true whatever the suffering. The suffering could be for Christ's sake; it could be the direct result of some sin; or it may be simply part of all the suffering that we are heir to as members of a fallen human race, and from which Christians are not exempt. It may be obviously great or apparently small, long-lasting or short; it is still real suffering. This is not only true of individuals, it is true of the church. Times of persecution and suffering have always been times of growth. Paul wrote, 'Suffering produces . . . character' (Rom 5:3-4). We know from what he said later that the character of which he is speaking is likeness to the Lord Jesus (Rom 8:29).

It is because, in God's hands, suffering is such an important factor in our growth into wholeness, that I want us to think about the way our suffering can be, and is, transformed by the Lord Jesus Christ. I am not attempting to solve the mystery of suffering. The subject is surrounded by mystery and only when we get to heaven will all our questions be answered. I just want to share some of what I do see in the Bible and also in the experience of Christians. While it will certainly not answer all our questions, it may help to bring us nearer to a place where we no longer need to have our questions answered, because we can trust.

The Bible is very real concerning human suffering

We see the beginning of human suffering in Genesis 3, a result of man's first act of disobedience; we see the end of human suffering in Revelation chapters 21 and 22, as a result of the final victory of the Lord Jesus. 'There will be no more . . . pain' (Rev 21:4). We are left in no doubt that the cause was man's sin and disobedience. The whole human race got off-centre; self-centred instead of God-centred, and that inevitably resulted in pain and suffering. The Bible is very clear that while the cause of the entry of suffering was man's sin, this does not mean that each person's suffering is necessarily directly related to some specific sin. Job's friends said that his suffering must have been caused by specific sin. Job cried out against this, and God affirmed that he was right and his friends wrong. When the disciples asked Jesus concerning a blind man, 'Rabbi, who sinned, this man or his parents, that he was born blind?' Jesus answered, 'Neither. . .' (Jn 9:2). From Adam and Eve onwards, the Bible tells us of all kinds of human suffering: physical, emotional, mental and spiritual. We see all kinds of bereavement and loss.

We see suffering in all kinds of human relationships; in families, in friendships and in other social and civil relationships. Man is not only alienated from God, he is alienated from man. We read of isolation and loneliness; of disappointment, depression, distress and despair. We read of oppression and slavery. We read of the suffering which results from great catastrophes—war, famine and earthquakes. We read of words being used as weapons to destroy instead of being a means of healing and reconciliation. We see the people of God suffering as well as those who do not know him. I could go on painting a very dark picture of all the human suffering woven into the Bible story. I am not doing it with the desire to depress us all, but to bring out in greater brightness the wonder of what we shall look at under the next two headings.

Our suffering entered into by God

From the beginning to the end of the Old Testament, we see a God who is not aloof, but is involved and active in the human situation, and in all human suffering. To use human terms, God did not say, 'They've decided to be independent of me, now they must get on with it; I wash my hands of them.' He is calling to them in the Garden of Eden, 'Where are you?' (Gen 3:9). He is calling them out of their hiding place. He is asking Cain, 'Where is your brother?' (Gen 4:9). He is reasoning with Cain, he is pleading with Cain, he even puts a mark on Cain so that others will not kill him (Gen 4:15).

Let us jump to the book of Exodus, where we read of God's people in cruel slavery in Egypt. Listen to him talking to Moses: 'I have indeed seen the misery of my people in Egypt. I have heard them crying out because of their slave drivers, and I am concerned about their suffering. So I have come down to rescue them from the hand of the Egyptians' (Ex 3:7-8).

If we move on to the Prophets, we realize that their very existence is a proof of God's entering into, and activity in, the human situation. Through them God reasons with his people and pleads with his people. Even when their suffering is the result of his judgement for their sin, he is showing that his greatest longing is that through their suffering they will return to him. Looking back to the years of suffering in Egypt Isaiah says, 'In all their distress he too was distressed, and the angel of his presence saved them' (Is 63:9). In Jeremiah and Hosea we see, more than in any other of the prophets, the heartbreak of God because of the suffering of his people brought about by their own sin. Jeremiah, echoing in his own heart the heart of God, sobs out, 'For the wound of the daughter of my people is my heart wounded' (Jer 8:21 RSV). Through Hosea God cries out, 'How can I give you up, Ephraim? How can I hand you over, Israel? . . . My heart is changed within me; all my compassion is aroused' (Hos 11:8).

It is not only his own people's suffering he enters into, and in which he is active. In the book of Jonah, we find him active in the affairs of Nineveh, capital city of Assyria, the nation that had brought great suffering to his people. God had sent Jonah to warn the people of Nineveh that if they did not repent of their sins, the city would be destroyed. When at last Jonah did preach that message, the people repented, God had compassion on them, and they were not destroyed. Jonah was angry. *He* did not want their ancient enemy to be saved. His view of God's mercy and compassion was too small; he thought it should only be active towards his own special people, not towards the other nations. In God's final rebuke of Jonah he said, 'Nineveh has more than a hundred and twenty thousand people who cannot tell their right hand from their left, and many cattle as well. Should I not be concerned about that great city?' (Jon 4:11).

Not only do we see God in the Old Testament constantly active in the suffering of the human race, but we also get glimpses of what he is working towards. He is wrestling with the human situation so as to bring about something even more wonderful than at the beginning. He intends to end suffering by removing the cause, and he is actually using the suffering to bring that about. Isaiah 35 is one of the chapters in which the prophet sees the end: 'Gladness and joy will overtake them, and sorrow and sighing will flee away' (v. 10).

If the Old Testament gives this clear picture of our God, the New Testament makes it more gloriously clear in the Person of our Lord Jesus Christ. 'Then Jesus came,' writes Matthew (3:13). God in human form. As soon as he began his public work, he started to attack actively all that caused human suffering: Satan, sin, sickness, death. G. Campbell Morgan, writing on the words of Mark, 'he could not stay hidden' (Mk 7:24 GNB), says:

From human suffering God cannot withdraw Himself, He cannot be hidden. It appeals to Him irresistably because of the grace of His nature . . . As He comes forth from His hiding-place, compelled by human agony, He comes to make no terms with that which has caused the pain; but He comes to end the pain by removing the cause.[18]

Raymond Brown, writing on the passage in Hebrews which speaks of Christ suffering and sharing our humanity says:

It is obvious from these verses that Christ took upon himself our humanity in all its suffering. Becoming man, he entered directly and personally into the arena of our anguish.[19]

Moreover, he himself suffered. In that second chapter of Hebrews, the writer tells us that 'he suffered death'; he was made 'perfect through suffering'; 'he himself suffered when he was tempted' (Heb 2:9-10,18). Later, he tells us that 'he learned obedience from what he suffered' (Heb 5:8). The Lord Jesus knows what we feel like, because he suffered all the limitations of being truly human. He suffered physically and mentally. He suffered misunderstanding, rejection, hostility and injustice. He suffered ridicule, scoffing and shame. He suffered the pain of words being used against him. He suffered in his relationships: his family thought he was mad; his own people cast him out; his disciples forsook him and one betrayed him. He suffered in his relationship with God, his Father. What more appalling loneliness and dereliction could there be than that which is expressed in his cry from the cross: 'My God, my God, why have you forsaken me?' (Mt 27:46).

In that wonderful chapter of Isaiah which has been fulfilled in the sufferings of Christ we read that he was 'familiar with suffering'; and later: 'He was pierced for our transgressions, he was crushed for our iniquities, the punishment that brought us peace was upon him . . . the Lord has laid on him the iniquity of us all' (Is 53:3,5-6). Peter, referring to this passage, sums it up by saying, 'He himself bore our sins in his body on the tree' (1 Pet 2:24).

To what greater depths than this could he have gone, in order to wrestle with human suffering and its cause, coming up victorious over all, opening the path through which our suffering can be transformed.

In the book of Revelation, the Lord Jesus Christ is on the throne, actively carrying out God's purposes until we read those words, 'No more death or mourning or crying or pain . . . No longer will there be any curse. . .' (Rev 21:4; 22:3).

All this is the measure of his infinite love for us.

Our suffering transformed by Christ

'Jesus Christ is the same yesterday and today and for ever' (Heb 13:8). As he was then so he is now. He enters into and is actively involved in all our suffering, whatever its cause, transforming what might be destructive into that which actually builds up. In what ways does he do this in the experience of Christians, so that while the suffering is still present, he changes the way they experience it, and uses it to bring about good? While there are no easy ways or pat answers, I would like to suggest certain very real ways:

His presence with us changes our experience of suffering

Sometimes there is a heightened awareness of his presence, so that the one who is suffering feels that the Lord Jesus is so near that if he or she just put out a hand, he could be touched. On these occasions, there is the felt comfort of the presence of One who perfectly understands and knows how we feel, and who feels with us. But it is not always so. Sometimes, the Christian grapples with a feeling of his absence rather than his presence, and it is only on looking back that he or she knows that he was there, and can see some of the ways in which his presence made a difference. When in the depths of a depressive illness, the feeling I experienced was of his absence. But, looking back, I could see with wonder that at the very time I felt he was absent, he was in fact most present, and was at work in the depths of my personality.

George Goodman described this experience in a poem:

The Footprints

He led me to the way of pain,
    A barren and a starless place.
(I did not know His eyes were wet,
    He would not let me see His face.)

He left me like a frightened child
    Unshielded in a night of storm.
(How should I dream He was so near,
    The rain-swept darkness hid His form.)

But when the clouds were driving back
    And dawn was breaking into day,
I knew Whose feet had walked with mine,
    I saw the footprints all the way.

I wonder if this poem sprang out of Psalm 77? There the psalmist starts by describing his suffering. Later on he pictures a tremendous storm and towards the end says, 'Your path led through the sea, your way through the mighty waters, though your footprints were not seen' (v.19). No, not at the time; but looking back they can be seen.

When Daniel's three friends were thrown into the

burning fiery furnace, I do not know whether they were aware of the presence of that fourth one who was with them. I do know that those outside the furnace saw his presence. It may be that in our suffering we have not experienced any special awareness of his presence, but others, perhaps some who are not Christians, have realized the difference that presence has made.

His presence in us changes our experience of suffering

The Lord Jesus is not only with us, he is in us. He is active in us in all our suffering. It is still true that in all our distress he is distressed. He feels with us, he perfectly understands what is going on inside us. No one else has that perfect inner knowledge of us. We may feel that he is not active, that he is doing nothing about the outer circumstances which cause the suffering. Can we change our view and look, not at the outer circumstances, but at what he is wanting to do inside us? His most vital activity is within us, using the very circumstances of suffering to cause growth and increasing likeness to himself.

One of the greatest qualities he works in us is *the ability to drop the demand to understand*, and to trust him with the unexplained. In the Bible, Job is an example of a man who suffered greatly and who cried out to God for an explanation (as all our human hearts tend to cry out). God never gave him that explanation, but he brought him to a place of peace and trust in an all-wise Creator-God, who knows what he is doing.

W. E. Sangster tells the following story:

I remember that when I was a small boy it was arranged one year that I should go on a fortnight's holiday with my school chums, and that no grown-up people should come with us. To our youthful minds the arrangement seemed ideal. . . . On the night before the holiday began, I counted up my pocket-money and came to the conclusion that it was not enough! So I went to father about it. He heard my reasoning with a quizzical smile, and murmured something about my ignorance of the value of money, but I left quite cheerfully with an understanding in *my* mind that a Postal Order would reach me during the second week. And in three days I was ready for the Postal Order, so I sent off a Post Card to accelerate it. I do not now remember what I put on the card, but I know the kind of card it was—'Dear Dad, S.O.S., L.S.D., R.S.V.P.' But this was the queer thing. No answer came. The first week ended and still no answer. The second began, and slipped away, and still no answer. My chums noticed my pre-occupation, and began to explain the absence of the Postal Order in their own way. One said, 'He has forgotten you're here.' I knew that was a lie. I knew my Dad. Another said: 'He's too busy to bother with a boy like you.' I knew that was a lie also. A third one said: 'What do you think yourself?' I did not know what to think. It was all mystery to me. 'I'll wait till I get home,' I said, 'and he'll tell me himself.'

There the small boy was able to let the matter rest until he returned home, when his father's love shone through the explanation he received. He goes on to say that that experience had been a parable to him. He describes a situation of great suffering in his family, then ends the story by saying,

I was dumb as a boy and I am dumb as a man. Some light shines upon these dark problems but no complete solution is at hand. I give to enquirers the answer which I gave to my school-mates years ago: 'I'll wait till I get home and He'll tell me Himself.' [20]

There comes a great transformation in the experience of suffering when he brings us to the place of trust which is content to echo these words.

I sometimes suspect that one look into his face and we shall not want or need explanations, because we shall see his infinite love for us in a way that we can only glimpse now.

He also works in us to produce a characteristic that is sometimes translated in the New Testament as *patience*, sometimes *perseverance* and sometimes *endurance*.

I quoted Paul as saying, 'Suffering produces . . . character.' I shall now fill in those dots! Paul supplies a step between the suffering and the character. He says, 'Suffering produces endurance, and endurance produces character' or, it could be 'Suffering produces patience, and patience produces character' (Rom 5:3-4 RSV). It does not matter which word we use, so long as we realize that it is not a passive word, it is an active one. It does not describe the kind of giving in which causes us to say, 'Oh well, I suppose I've got to accept this and put up with it till God sees fit to bring me through it.' It describes an active taking hold of the situation with the intention of walking through it with God, of learning from it, of seeing it turned to a positive good in one's life.

A young man going through a time of suffering and testing of his faith said, 'I do know that one thing God is producing in me is patience.'

There was an active expectation that God was teaching him and causing him to grow as a result of the experience.

James, writing of all kinds of suffering and trial, says, 'Realise that they come to test your faith and to produce in you the quality of endurance. But let the process go on until that endurance is fully developed, and you will find you have become men of mature character with the right sort of independence' (Jas 1:2-4 PHILLIPS).

The greatest example in all history of this characteristic is the Lord Jesus himself 'who for the joy set before him endured the cross, scorning its shame' (Heb 12:2). He took hold of that which could have been the greatest defeat and turned it into the greatest victory the world has ever known. And he lives in us to make it possible for us to walk through our experiences of suffering in such a way that they will not be times of defeat but of victory. In particular, victory as regards the strengthening of our faith, and the growth towards maturity and likeness to Jesus.

The quality of active patience or endurance also has a very healthy effect in driving out bitterness, resentment, self-pity, frustration and other destructive factors which we have repeatedly seen to hinder growth, and which so easily creep in during times of suffering. As the Lord works in us something of his own patient endurance, there will not be much room left for those destructive factors.

His purpose in our suffering

Not only his presence with us and in us, but also the knowledge that he has a purpose in our suffering, changes our experience of that suffering.

Often, our hearts cry out that it all seems so meaningless; if only we could see some purpose. When our almighty and loving Lord allows us to go through times of suffering, he will take the very stuff of which the suffering is formed and use it to fulfil his own purposes for us. Those purposes are always towards life, growth and healing. And so he really does turn the curse into a blessing (Neh 13:2). Once again, it is often only on looking back that we are able to see something of what his purpose has been. For a Christian, even if his purpose cannot be seen, the knowledge that there is a purpose, and a purpose of love, makes a great difference. It is the feeling of being trapped in purposeless suffering which leads many to despair. For the Christian, suffering is never that kind of trap, it is more like a path which is going somewhere.

Many Christians have said that suffering has been the means of their getting a different perspective on things; the ability to see from a different point of view, to begin to see as God sees rather than from our limited vision. It can clear and enlarge our vision as regards God's purposes, God's values, God's character. I am not denying that sometimes suffering actually limits our vision for a while—we can see nothing but the suffering. It is as we enter into our suffering with the Lord, and are real and open with him about our feelings, that the time comes when vision clears and is enlarged.

> This small and temporary trouble we suffer will bring us a tremendous and eternal glory, much greater than the trouble. For we fix our attention, not on things that are seen, but on things that are unseen. What can be seen lasts only for a time, but what cannot be seen lasts for ever (2 Cor 4:17-18 GNB).

What God works in us through suffering is that which lasts for ever.

There are times when the purpose of pain is to remove another kind of pain. One spring, when I was a girl, I was thrown off my bike by skidding on a newly tarred and gravelled part of the road. The result was nasty grazes on the palms of my hands, with gravel embedded in the wounds. When I got home, my father was there. One look at my hands and he took me up to the bathroom. He picked up a scrubbing brush, told me that what he was going to do would hurt, and then gently but firmly removed all the gravel! It certainly hurt, but I let him do it because I trusted my father and knew he loved me. When the wounds were clean, he put on something soothing and bandaged my hands. After that, I don't think there was any problem with the healing. He may have used a crude method, but I knew that the purpose of the pain he caused me was to get rid of that which would have encouraged the ongoing pain of festering wounds rather than the healing of clean ones.

I have seen people with what I call festering wounds in their personalities. The wound never heals because hidden away there is bitterness, resentment and perhaps guilt, in spite of the knowledge of God's forgiveness. The guilt is frequently caused by self-condemnation which has continued to be mixed up with the pain. Then the Lord allows some suffering to come into that person's life, and the present suffering brings up all the old pain, bitterness and guilt. These are now brought to the Lord for him to take away, so that the old wound becomes a clean wound.

I think of a Christian woman whose little girl died at the age of six. She and others thought she had got over the bereavement wonderfully. Sixteen years later, she suffered the bereavement of both her parents within a short space of time. The pain of those bereavements brought back all the pain connected with the sickness and death of her little girl. She lived it all over again, constantly weeping and unable to get all the details out of her mind. Gradually, she was able to open up the old wound to the Lord and became aware that there had been resentment and guilt which she had never got rid of. She brought it all to him, asking for his forgiveness and cleansing, and knew that a deep healing was taking place. The wound was still tender, but the pain was now the pain of a healing wound, no longer that of a festering wound.

Don't forget that his purposes are wider than just in

the person who is suffering. He has purposes in those who are round about. In a church where one person is going through a known experience of suffering, God has purposes in that church. Purposes of growth, of learning, of understanding. Perhaps purposes of drawing together in closer fellowship, of teaching lessons about prayer. And one of God's purposes in the person who is suffering is that that one will be equipped to help others in their suffering. When we have experienced God's comfort in our particular time of suffering, we discover that we are not only equipped to help others going through a similar time of suffering, but those who are going through *any* time of suffering. Paul is saying this in 2 Corinthians 1:3-4, '. . . the God of all comfort, who comforts us in all our troubles, so that we can comfort those in any trouble with the comfort we ourselves have received from God.'

His victory changes our experience of suffering

Lastly, the victory of the Lord Jesus Christ over death changes the Christian's experience of suffering.

By his resurrection from the dead, the Lord Jesus ensured for us a glorious life beyond death in which there will be no more suffering and pain. The New Testament glows with the certainty of our resurrection life with the Lord. The final answer is never seen to be in this limited life on earth—but there, beyond, in the unending joy of heaven, our true home. However much we may experience in this life of his healing for our bodies, one day they will die, unless Jesus comes first. The final answer for our bodies is in the perfect resurrection bodies he will give us. However much we grow into being like Jesus, which must be our constant aim, John tells us that it is only when we see him face to face, as he is, that that likeness will be complete (1 Jn 3:2).

It is this hope that has transformed the sufferings of

countless Christians all down the ages, and seems to shine brightest in times of persecution. Paul says, 'In my opinion whatever we may have to go through now is less than nothing compared with the magnificent future God has planned for us' (Rom 8:18 PHILLIPS). His victory over death includes victory over all the power of Satan and his destructive forces. This we can claim in this life, so that our times of suffering do not become destructive, but constructive times of growth. His victory over death and Satan is not only our final hope as individuals, it is also the real hope for this suffering, agonizing world. A day is coming when God will again break into human history, the Lord Jesus will return and bring about those conditions which we read of particularly in the book of Revelation, when ' . . . the old order of things has passed away' and, 'There will be no more death or mourning or crying or pain' (Rev 21:4).

In the chapel of St Julian's Community in Sussex (a lovely place of rest and refreshment), there is a wide plain glass window behind the communion table. Beyond that window is part of the garden. Hanging in front of the centre of the window, and looking as if it is a part of the window, is a metal framework in the shape of a cross, thus making it possible to see through the cross to the garden beyond. One spring, a young woman who was going through a great deal of suffering, wrote a poem sitting in that chapel which was a significant part of a healing, growing process in her. With her permission, I quote that poem:

> He knows—
> Whose feet once trod this earth
> The pain of birth—
> through life—
> to birth again.

He chose—
The pathway to the Cross
Knowing his loss—
    would one day—
      be my gain.

He rose—
The Cross naught but a frame
The shell of pain.
    —look through
      —and see new life
        —blossom again.

To me that sums up what I have been seeking to say.

The cross is central. On that cross, the Lord Jesus summed up all God's love and all God's activity in history. Identifying himself with us, taking into himself our sin, the basic cause of all our suffering.

Now the cross is empty. In front of it, on the table, are the symbols of his death; the bread and wine, reminders of his body broken for us, his blood shed for us. Through that cross, we can see a garden and the springing up of new life, reminding us of his glorious resurrection and victory over all the power of sin and death and Satan. We know that it is through this pathway that he made possible, for all who know him, the transformation of their suffering. He is alive, still sharing and actively at work in our suffering. It may still take the shape of a cross, but that is now the shell of pain through which we can see new life and therefore new growth blossoming again.

8

EPILOGUE

Three Schools in Which We Grow

I have used the word 'schools' because, from our side, growing is very much a learning process. Learning about God; his love, his purposes, his ways. Learning about the Lord Jesus Christ and all that he makes possible for us. Learning from the Holy Spirit, about whom Jesus said that he 'will teach' (Jn 14:26). Learning about ourselves. Learning God's principles of growth and learning how these may become real in our experience.

I have mentioned these three schools in passing, in previous chapters, but want now to close by identifying them separately.

The school of solitude

We need time to be alone with the Lord. Time to be quiet in his presence. Time to be still and know that he is God (Ps 46:10). We need time alone to pour out our hearts to him (Ps 62:8). Time to pour out to him all our problems, our troubles, our distressed feelings as well as our praise and thanksgiving. We need time for private prayer; to talk to him about people and situations in a way which would not be possible in the presence of anyone else. We need time alone with our Bibles to meditate on what we read and to seek to listen to him.

Paul wrote, 'We, who with unveiled faces all reflect the Lord's glory, are being transformed into his likeness with ever-increasing glory, which comes from the Lord, who is the Spirit' (2 Cor 3:18).

He had been speaking about people reading the Old Testament with veils covering their hearts. Those veils are taken away when we turn to Christ. Our 'inner eyes' are opened so that we begin to see the glory of the Lord in the Scriptures.

As we read the Old Testament, we can see the glory of the Lord in creation, in his dealings with individuals and in the history of his people. Increasingly, his character shines out, perhaps particularly in the Psalms and the Prophets. In the New Testament, we have a clearer vision of his glory in the Lord Jesus. We see the glory of God in the life, the death and the resurrection of Jesus. In the Acts and in the letters written by Paul and others, we see the glory of God in our risen, living Saviour and Lord. In the last book of the Bible, we get a glimpse of the final, totally unclouded glory of the Lord, still shining out in majestic splendour in our Lord Jesus. This vision takes us to that time when John says, 'We shall be like him, for we shall see him as he is' (1 Jn 3:2). Our part is to contemplate that glory. While we contemplate, we are being transformed into the likeness of our Lord Jesus by his Spirit.

There are some for whom it is almost impossible to find time and place to be alone with the Lord, but the Lord will give ideas when, realizing their need, they ask him to guide them as to where and when they can meet with him. For instance, some have found that being alone in the car driving to work can be an opportunity to praise the Lord and pray for others. Of course, the Bible can't be read, but it is possible to listen to cassettes.

Once I recorded a passage from the Bible on tape and listened to it while driving. Others have found a church building a place where they can, at some time of the day, be alone with the Lord. The car or the church may not be right for you, they are just examples of what others have found. It is often very difficult for mothers during the years of bringing up small children to find a regular time and place—I certainly found it so—but the Lord does give ideas when we ask him. Don't condemn yourself though if during those years it can't be very regular.

The school of fellowship

Paul, in his prayer in Ephesians 3, says that it is with all the saints that we get to know the greatness of Christ's love. Some years ago, a missionary was asked to give Bible readings at a Christian convention overseas. He held an important position of responsibility in his Mission. At that time, the Mission did not feel it right to have fellowship with any but those within its own ranks. He was very exercised about this and finally decided that he must accept the invitation, even if it meant losing his position. At that convention, he enjoyed rich fellowship with Christians from many different denominations and missions. When it was over, he said that the great lesson he had learned was that if we are not open to fellowship with other Christians, we shall be limited in our knowledge of the love of Christ. We deprive ourselves and we deprive them. We need the fellowship of other Christians that, together, we may grow by that nourishment which we all supply to one another.

How glorious if that fellowship can break through the barriers of denomination, of colour, of culture, of sex and of age. Surely Paul was thinking of this when he wrote, 'Here there is no Greek or Jew, circumcised or uncircumcised, barbarian, Scythian, slave or free, but Christ is all, and is in all' (Col 3:11). 'Christ is all,' or, 'Christ is all that matters' (PHILLIPS). No doubt if Paul lived today he would be naming different categories of people from those he mentioned, but the principle would be the same.

That is the kind of fellowship in which we grow. If at all possible, we do need to grow in, and with, a local church fellowship. It is significant that all down the ages, the church's central act of worship has been the Communion Service, a service of fellowship where we remember that greatest demonstration of God's love, as we receive the broken bread and poured out wine, which speak of the death of the Lord Jesus.

Remember, too, that we can have rich fellowship with Christians of other places and other generations through Christian literature.

The school of life

By this, I mean all the circumstances which go to make up our lives in this world: our homes, our work, our recreation, and all our relationships; all that comes into our lives as a result of being part of the human race. This includes all the pressures from which we cannot escape while we journey through life. Added to all the pressures which are an inevitable part of life, Christians have the pressure of being in a spiritual conflict. It is good for us to be aware of this, and to ask the Lord to give us discernment to spot special times and ways in which Satan attacks. It is a mistake to get too taken up with this enemy of ours, and to give more time to thinking about him than about our victorious Lord. At the same time, it is important in our growing process to recognize him behind such things as accusation and condemnation. We should also be alert to the advantage he wants to take of our times of discouragement and failure.

In the school of life, it is God who is in control of all our circumstances. Satan complained to God that he had put a hedge round Job so that he couldn't touch him without God's permission! This is true of us. Nothing can touch us except God allows it; and if he allows it, then he will take hold of it and turn to our good; he will use it for our growth and increasing likeness to Jesus.

If we go back to the thought of the potter, we can rest in the certainty that he, our heavenly Potter, is in control of the wheel of circumstances wherever it touches us. He really is!

It may be that, by circumstances beyond our control, we are barred from one or more of these schools. Can we trust him that he is in control of *those* circumstances, and that he will make up to us in other ways so that our growth is not hindered?

If all three are open to us, let us use them all with thankfulness, knowing that, as we expose ourselves to his teaching, we shall learn and the result will be growth.

I should like to end by putting the emphasis where we began. Whether it is the Potter remaking us or the Teacher teaching us, it is *God* who makes things grow.

NOTES

1. R. C. Lucas, *Fullness and Freedom* (IVP 1980) p.125.
2. Ibid. p.42.
3. William Temple, *Readings in St John's Gospel* (Macmillan & Co. Ltd 1945) p.285.
4. R. C. Lucas, *Fullness and Freedom* (IVP 1980) p.151.
5. W. E. Sangster, *The Pure in Heart* (Epworth Press 1954) p.241.
6. H. R. Mackintosh, *The Christian Experience of Forgiveness* (Nisbet & Co. Ltd 1927) p.36.
7. J. H. Jowett, *Brooks by the Traveller's Way* (H. R. Allenson Ltd) p.25.
8. Source unknown.
9. Rita Nightingale, *Freed For Life* (Marshall, Morgan & Scott 1982) p.176.
10. Elizabeth Goudge, *The Joy of the Snow* (Coronet Edit. 1977, first pub. by H & S Ltd 1976) p.240.
11. Amy Carmichael, *Rose From Brier* (SPCK 1933) p.77.
12. Rev. Ralph P. Martin, *Epistle to the Philippians, Tyndale N.T. Commentaries* (Tyndale Press 1959 now IVP) p.178.
13. Roger Hurding, *As Trees Walking* (Paternoster Press 1982) p.204.

14. W. E. Sangster, *The Pure in Heart* (Epworth Press 1954) p.151.
15. William Hendriksen, *N.T. Commentary John* (Baker Book House, Grand Rapids, USA; Banner of Truth Trust 1954) p.155.
16. *New Bible Commentary Revised* (IVP 1970) p.345.
17. G. Campbell Morgan, *Gospel According to Matthew* (Oliphants Ltd) p.115.
18. G. Campbell Morgan, *Searchlights from the Word* (Pickering & Inglis Ltd) p.310.
19. Raymond Brown, *Christ Above All* (IVP 1982) p.56.
20. W. E. Sangster, *He Is Able* (Hodder & Stoughton 1936; Wyvern Books 1958) p.16.

God Wants You Whole
The Way to Healing, Health and Wholeness

by Selwyn Hughes

If God is always willing to heal, why do people remain ill—even when they have faith for healing?

How can we all live more healthy lives, day by day?

With openness and honesty, Selwyn Hughes faces squarely the issues of health and healing that concern every one of us. He examines the most common causes of ill health and the reasons we fail to receive God's healing grace. Here we see how our Creator has lovingly provided all we need for wholeness of living, if only we set ourselves to live in accordance with his will.

Above all, this book shows that even when healing eludes us and our condition is not remedied quickly, we can still rest secure in the knowledge that our heavenly Father is committed to our good—in spirit, mind, emotions, and body.

Also by Selwyn Hughes in Kingsway paperback:
A friend in Need; How to Live the Christian Life; The Christian Counsellor's Pocket Guide; Everyday Reflections; A New Heart; Marriage as God Intended.

Kingsway Publications

How to Fail Successfully

by Jill Briscoe

Failure is forgivable—not final

Does the fear of failure prevent you from stepping out in faith, or from witnessing to your family and friends?

Do those so-called 'little' sins rob you of the victory you know you should be enjoying in your Christian life?

Take heart, says Jill Briscoe—failure is not the end. Coping with failure, and learning to overcome it, are part of God's plan for all his children. Christians are not yet made, but in the making.

Jill Briscoe, in her own warm and witty style, gives practical insights and encouragement in her speaking and writing ministry around the world. She and her husband Stuart Briscoe, well known for their ministry in this country, now reside in the United States with their three children.

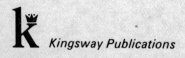

Kingsway Publications

Overcomers through the Cross

by Paul E. Billheimer

The work of the Holy Spirit in the life of the believer is both a crisis and a process. God's work in our hearts is not completed in a day.

If we want God's best for our lives, we need to recognize our own weakness. Even after being born again and filled with the holy Spirit, there are areas of our lives that must be continually yielded to the cross so that we may enjoy increasing power and victory.

This book helps us to put our faith into action learn what it really means to lose our own lives and so find abundant life in Christ.

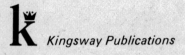
Kingsway Publications

I Believe

by Colin Day

What do Christians believe?

This book is a guide to the basic beliefs of the Christian faith as expressed in the Apostles' Creed.

Far more than a simple list of doctrines, it explores the practical implications of our beliefs, challenging us to a greater depth of Christian commitment in our day-to-day living.

A Falcon Book
Kingsway Publications